New Directions in Religion and Literature

Dante and the Sense of Transgression

New Directions in Religion and Literature

This series aims to showcase new work at the forefront of religion and literature through short studies written by leading and rising scholars in the field. Books will pursue a variety of theoretical approaches as they engage with writing from different religious and literary traditions. Collectively, the series will offer a timely critical intervention to the interdisciplinary crossover between religion and literature, speaking to wider contemporary interests and mapping out new directions for the field in the early twenty-first century.

Also Available From Bloomsbury:
Blake. Wordsworth. Religion, Jonathan Roberts
Do the Gods Wear Capes?, Ben Saunders
England's Secular Scripture, Jo Carruthers
Late Walter Benjamin, John Schad
The New Atheist Novel, Arthur Bradley and Andrew Tate
Victorian Parables, Susan E. Colón

Forthcoming:
Buddhism and Radical Poetics, Peter Jaeger
Faithful Reading, Mark Knight and Emma Mason
Glyph and the Gramophone, Luke Ferretter
Rewriting the Old Testament in Anglo-Saxon Verse, Samantha Zacher

Dante and the Sense of Transgression
'The Trespass of the Sign'

William Franke

BLOOMSBURY
LONDON · NEW DELHI · NEW YORK · SYDNEY

Bloomsbury Academic
An imprint of Bloomsbury Publishing Plc

50 Bedford Square	175 Fifth Avenue
London	New York
WC1B 3DP	NY 10010
UK	USA

www.bloomsbury.com

First published 2013

© William Franke, 2013

All rights reserved. No part of this publication may be reproduced or transmitted in any form or by any means, electronic or mechanical, including photocopying, recording, or any information storage or retrieval system, without prior permission in writing from the publishers.

William Franke has asserted his right under the Copyright, Designs and Patents Act, 1988, to be identified as Author of this work.

No responsibility for loss caused to any individual or organization acting on or refraining from action as a result of the material in this publication can be accepted by Bloomsbury Academic or the author.

British Library Cataloguing-in-Publication Data
A catalogue record for this book is available from the British Library.

ISBN: HB: 978-1-4411-3691-6
PB: 978-1-4411-6042-3

Library of Congress Cataloging-in-Publication Data
Franke, William.
Dante and the sense of transgression: the trespass of the sign/William Franke.
p. cm. – (New directions in religion and literature)
Includes bibliographical references and index.
ISBN 978-1-4411-6042-3 (pbk.) – ISBN 978-1-4411-3691-6 (hardcover) – ISBN 978-1-4411-5028-8 (PDF) – ISBN 978-1-4411-8502-0 (ePub) 1. Dante Alighieri, 1265-1321–Philosophy. 2. Dante Alighieri, 1265-1321. Paradiso. I. Title.

PQ4412.F73 2012
851'.1–dc23
2012011971

Typeset by Deanta Global Publishing Services, Chennai, India

A *ma* Béatrice
Nomina sunt consequentia rerum
(Dante, *Vita Nuova*, XIII.4)

Contents

Preface x
Introduction

1 Dante's Implication in the Transgressiveness
   He Condemns   3

Part 1 Language and Beyond

2 The Linguistic Turn of Transgression in the *Paradiso*   19
3 At the Limits of Language or Reading Dante
   through Blanchot   29
4 The Step/Not Beyond   35
5 The Neuter – Nothing Except Nuance   42
6 Forgetting and the Limits of Experience – *Letargo* and
   the *Argo*   47
7 Speech – The Vision that is Non-Vision   60
8 Writing – The 'Essential Experience'   76
9 The Gaze of Orpheus   83
10 Beatrice and Eurydice   89
11 Blanchot's Dark Gaze and the Experience of
   Literature as Transgression   95
12 Negative Theology and the Space of Literature – Order
   Beyond Order   98

Part 2 Authority and Powerlessness (Kenosis)

13 Necessary Transgression – Human versus
   Transcendent Authority   107
14 Dante and the Popes   110

15	Against the Emperor?	114
16	Inevitable Transgression along a Horizontal Axis	116
17	Heterodox Dante and Christianity	119
18	Christianity: An Inherently Transgressive Religion?	123

Part 3 Transgression and Transcendence

19	Transgression and the Sacred in Bataille and Foucault	134
20	Transgression as the Path to God – the Authority of Inner Experience	138
21	Transcendence and the Sense of Transgression	145

Appendix: Levinasian Transcendence and the Ethical Vision of the *Paradiso*	151
Notes	177
Index	197

. . . the only possible transgression of current order would be a theological one.

(John Milbank, *The Future of Love*)

The sign and divinity have the same time and place of birth. The epoch of the sign is essentially theological.

(Jacques Derrida, *De la grammatologie*)

Transgression deranges the promise of a beyond or the promise of an otherwise: it is an act, always active and for that reason unassignable, ungraspable otherwise than by that which it opposes. Making the immoveable squeak and upsetting the state of things, transgression never rests. That is why it needs to maintain that which it annuls, and why it aims not at the annihilation of its limit, but at rerouting it in other forms to another place. Transgressing is always exceeding but never achieving. It is bending without breaking, biting without consuming.

(Georges Bataille, 1958 interview, translated from sound recording)

Preface

In 2009, I was invited by Paivi Methonen on behalf of the Nordic Dante Network to give the keynote address for the Fourth Interdisciplinary Conference on 'Dante and Transgression'. It was not a topic that immediately appealed to me, but it proved highly productive for stimulating development in a new direction of my long-deferred project for an interpretation of Dante's *Paradiso* based on contemporary thinking especially of French provenance. That the philosophy of difference could be used to elucidate, in terms addressed to our own time and intellectual horizon, the nature of poetic language as theological revelation in the final movement of Dante's epic and prophetic poem is a conviction I had been gestating ever since the publication in 1996 of *Dante's Interpretive Journey* in a series on 'Religion and Postmodernism' at the University of Chicago Press.

According to its manuscript subtitle (lost in the process of publication), this earlier book proposes *A Hermeneutical Dialogue between the Divine Comedy and Modern Thought*. It outlines a hermeneutic theory – indeed an existential theory of interpretation as inherently and inseparably philosophical, theological and poetic – in the form of a theoretically reflective interpretation of Dante's *Divine Comedy*. It draws on and, at the same time, critiques predominantly German hermeneutic thinking as it flourishes in Heidegger and Gadamer, with reference also to Schleiermacher, Dilthey, Ebeling, Fuchs, Bultmann and Ricoeur, in a reading of the theologically revelatory interpretative structure and dynamic of Dante's poetic vision. The poem is approached speculatively as an event of theological truth in and through interpretative acts of the reader, whose interventions are expressly invited and enjoined by the remarkable and indeed revolutionary addresses to the reader. These addresses, in effect, frame everything that happens in the poem within the horizon of the reader's understanding and interpretation of it. The reader's own existence and life journey are thereby called upon to actively determine the meaning of the poem by personal appropriation and application. Reading becomes an act of self-examination and a search for self-understanding in the revelatory light shed by each of the figures represented in the poem. This dynamic dimension of reading is incorporated programmatically – through the addresses – into the text itself and its modalities of generating meaning.

This first book's readings happen to concentrate on and are practically confined to passages from the *Inferno* and the *Purgatorio*. Although it argues for an existential-hermeneutical interpretation of the *Divine Comedy* as a whole, *Dante's Interpretive Journey* contains no substantial or detailed readings of extended passages from the *Paradiso*. The hermeneutic paradigm worked perfectly for the first two parts of Dante's tripartite masterpiece, but the third part turns out to be very different in its intellectual bearings and spiritual underpinnings. It became apparent along the way that a substantially different theoretical paradigm would be necessary to adequately construe the poem's final movement in philosophical terms today, for the *Paradiso* moves beyond interpretation and beyond language. In the last part of his poem, Dante butts up against the limits of his whole project and of writing and language *tout court*. The universal synthetic vision, which he has so superbly constructed, in crucial ways comes undone. Indeed, this very undoing becomes the vehicle of the quest's fulfilment. Not everything can be digested by poetic methods of interpretation or by theological concepts. What is *beyond interpretation* becomes Dante's central, or rather seminal, obsession in this final portion of his poetic odyssey. Symptomatic of this predicament is that the *Paradiso* is inflected, from beginning to end, by the ineffability topos.

'Beyond language' and 'beyond interpretation' are likewise central preoccupations of a style of critical thinking that, as much as hermeneutic thought, has indelibly marked contemporary culture. Primarily of French rather than of Germanic extraction, this alternative and very often adversarial critical approach pivots on the notion of 'difference' – specifically on the postulate that meaning originates in difference rather than in self-significant being or in anything that is intrinsically itself and the same. Not achieving understanding by reduction to identity through fusion in a universal horizon, but rather defending particular differences from effacement and provoking recognition of the irreducibly Other, count among this current's most urgent concerns.

Of course, in practice, beneath all rhetorically exhibited antagonisms, the two approaches tend to mix and are deeply inter-dependent and even inseparable from each other. Nevertheless, their divergent directions and emphases and agendas serve to articulate a distinction of type between the theoretical paradigm explored by the present book and that elaborated by *Dante's Interpretive Journey*. The shift in the theoretical infrastructure of Dante's own project, as he moves into the *Paradiso*, demands this modulation of the paradigms employed for interpretation of the philosophical stakes of the *Commedia*: such a shift corresponds to the poem's transition from the terrestrial climb completed in earthly Paradise or Eden at the top of the mountain of Purgatory to the ascent through the spheres of heavenly Paradise, reaching finally to the immaterial Empyrean beyond time and space and representation altogether.

Consequently, the theoretical issues that the last part of the poem raises and the philosophical thinking that it embodies in poetic practice require different tools to be dealt with effectively. The topos of 'ineffability' and its correlative negative or apophatic theology scan the *Paradiso* from beginning to end and become key to an appropriate theoretical framing of this sublimest portion of the *Divine Comedy*. A 'negative poetics' here decisively qualifies and delimits – yet also frees and fulfils – Dante's poetics of revelation. French deconstructive theory and philosophy of difference are peculiarly apt for providing the theoretical terms for a contemporary understanding of this last turning in Dante's work, which in decisive ways turns out to be the work's own self-dismantling. At this stage, Dante's journey to God becomes practically identified with the journey constituted by the writing of the poem itself: the literary journey now shadows (and in some sense *over*shadows) Dante's flight through the planetary and stellar – and finally empyreal – heavens. Paradoxically, in this shifting light, the poem in the end outshines itself, and something altogether beyond the linguistic and even the human comes to pass. The paradox is that this glimpse beyond is opened up by an ever greater concentration on language – to the point where it disappears *as language*, transgressing its status as sign and becoming a sort of reality in its own right and finally a passage beyond reality as we know it.

In this manner, then, the present book complements its predecessor. It rounds out my reading of the literary-critical and metaphysical-epistemological stakes of the *Commedia* through the lenses of contemporary thought and critical theory. And yet my critical work on the *Paradiso* is, with this book, still only very partially complete. My more detailed readings of particular passages of the *Paradiso* remain reserved for a separate volume, which has evolved under the working title of *The Veil of Eternity: Language and Transcendence in Dante's Paradiso*. A few fragments of it, meanwhile, have become available in preliminary form in periodical publications that are referenced in the text.

This distribution of my work on Dante's final poetic testament permits me to present the theoretical framework for dealing with the *Paradiso* principally in the present volume and to concentrate on detailed exegesis of key passages of the poem in a negative theological vein in the sequel. The close reading of Dante's poem has not been taken up here, except rarely. The work in hand attempts to deal with theoretical issues raised by the poem, yet exegesis and theory remain vital to each other and consequently the manuscripts interlock. Taken together, they aim to illuminate the extraordinary feat of the *Paradiso*, in which Dante's invention of poetic language as theological revelation culminates.

It is crucial to my approach to the *Paradiso* to link the medieval intellectual background of negative or apophatic theology with its contemporary analogues in the corresponding forms of culture that we are at present struggling to assimilate. I am committed to pursuing the study of Dante not just as a philological exercise but as a philosophical challenge and even as a means of interrogating our most fundamental beliefs, particularly our religious and ethical-political convictions, together with their epistemological and metaphysical correlates. This approach enables us to discern at work in Dante's poem an event of truth and perhaps even a step beyond 'truth' and other such concepts – with concomitant questioning of the very possibility and limits of conceptualization. This discernment participates in the event inaugurated by Dante's poem, which plays itself out and achieves its destiny in the history of human culture by realizing itself in contemporary consciousness.

This sort of continuing event of critical and theoretical reflection pursued by means of interdisciplinary inquiry is exemplary of what I take to be one of the most challenging aspects of the recent resurgence of scholarly investigation in the field of religion and literature, to which this volume also intends to contribute. In 2010, I was invited by Emma Mason and Mark Knight to publish a short monograph in the Continuum series on New Directions in Literature and Religion. This invitation (followed up by their generous critical reading) provided the opportunity to turn the fruits of the aforementioned presentation to the Nordic Dante Network into a book focused on some provocative theoretical aspects of Dante's ultimate and most demanding poetic achievement. Yet another challenge coming from Maurice Sprague and Ben Pohl – to give a keynote speech for the 2011 Deutsche Forschung Gemeinschaft (DFG) Ancient and Medieval Colloquium on 'Erfahren, Erzählen, Errinern' ('Record, Relate, Remember') at the Otto-Friedrich University of Bamberg – proved invaluable for sounding out material on '*Letargo* and the Argo: Total Forgetting as the Moment of Truth at the Climax of Dante's *Divine Comedy* and the Christian Epic Tradition'. Further benefits accrued from a seminar on 'Dante e la teologia negativa' that I was privileged to give at the bidding of Andrea Aguti and Piergiorgio Grassi at the *Istituto Superiore di Scienze Religiose* of the Carlo Bo University of Urbino. I gratefully acknowledge and thank all involved for their initiatives, including finally Marion Ciréfice and *L'association saute frontière* for an idyllic residency in the French *Haut Jura*. Translations from other languages into English are my own.

Maison de la Poésie Transjurassienne
Cinquétral (St Claude)
January–May 2011

Introduction

1

Dante's Implication in the Transgressiveness He Condemns

We are accustomed to viewing Dante's poetic masterpiece, *The Divine Comedy*, as a bastion of orthodox Christian belief and as the impassioned expression of an authoritarian political doctrine. Dante indeed portrays himself as a Knight of Faith humbly obedient to heaven and zealously intent upon establishing one Kingdom under God on earth. He positions himself as a militant member of the Catholic Church, which stands under the authority of one head, Christ, represented by his 'vicar', the Pope, to whom unconditional obedience in all matters spiritual is due. He is an equally uncompromising champion of the God-given right of the Holy Roman Empire, according it unlimited jurisdiction over all secular affairs and ascribing absolute power in this arena again to a single individual, the Emperor. Whether he looks at the sacred or the secular spheres, Dante envisages a perfectly unified order commanded from above and comprehending the whole domain of human freedom, with no allowances made for any dissension whatsoever. 'Dante and transgression' might at first sight appear to be a misconceived or a meager topic, unless it means to investigate Dante's apparent *suppression* of all transgression.

Dante is, in fact, ruthless against all who transgress the purportedly universal moral and theological order he advocated as alone right and just. *The Divine Comedy* sternly condemns a whole spectrum of heresies, exemplarily Arianism and Sabellianism (*Par.* XIII.127), reviling virtually any departure from the authoritative doctrine of the Roman Catholic Church. It blesses Folquet of Marseille (*Par.* IX.20), in spite of the fact that he was the pitiless persecutor of the Cathars, cruelly doing to death this peace-loving, refined civilization, which served as fertile seedbed for some of the most exultant triumphs of the troubadour poetry that Dante himself admired and emulated. Dante also celebrates Saint Dominic for his vigorous action in rooting out heretics (*sterpi eretici* – heretical shoots) by nipping in the bud all forms of heterodoxy (*Par.* XII.97–102). This was the spirit of rigour that became the animus of the Inquisition in trials conducted in subsequent centuries by the Dominican Order. The poem takes hostile stances towards those in odour of suspicion, such as the spiritual Franciscans. It censures their leader, Ubertino da Casale (*Par.* XII.124) and issues a warning to Fra Dolcino (*Inf.* XXVIII.55–60), head of the Apostolic Brethren, who in their attempt to return to apostolic purity and austerity were likewise perceived as a threat by the ecclesiastical hierarchy in Rome.

Dante is no less severe against those transgressing the secular world order as he construes it. He makes examples of Brutus and Cassius – seen devoured in the mouths of Satan at the bottom of Hell for having rebelled against Caesar. As a prophet of world government, Dante envisions a regime that would require all to submit to one supreme head and brook no disobedience. Any attempted transgression against this order is to be thoroughly eradicated and avenged. The tortures of the Hell Dante created are a chilling witness to his firm determination that all who transgress what he takes to be the divine ordinance for the world should be tormented without mercy or surcease. On all these counts, Dante seems to be totally intolerant of transgression in any form and hell-bent on punishing anyone who dares to differ.

At the same time, Dante's very obsession with avoiding and repressing transgression betrays an unmistakable sense of his own deeply and ineradicably transgressive desires. This is patent already in his boundless artistic ambition. We find him pushing the limits of existing styles and genres and deliberately going further in every respect of his poetic art than any of his predecessors. His career is marked by its transgression of the conventional norms for vernacular poetry and by his competitive drive to rival and surpass even the ancients, exceeding all established codes and canons.[1] It is difficult to overlook a cantankerous penchant to transgressiveness that invests all Dante's most characteristic attitudes and acts. The *Epistolae* deliver important testimony on this head, notably those addressed defiantly to the *signori* governing Florence and to the cardinals of Italy.[2] A truculent and combative personality he surely was, and just this character is inscribed into his poem, not least in its abundance of strident polemics and diatribes.

The poem, moreover, is riddled with paradoxical exceptions that transgress the totalitarian order it otherwise seems to affirm: it turns on surprises, such as the meeting with Cato of Utica as Gate-keeper of Purgatory. As a pagan suicide and opponent of Caesar, he should have been excluded from salvation. And what astonishment again attends the discovery of the pagan hero, Riphaeus Troianus, together with Roman Emperor Trajan, among the souls of the blessed in Paradise! All had apparently lived and died without the necessary faith and saving grace of Christ. Dante flaunts such encounters as apparently flagrant transgressions against the assumed law of 'no salvation outside of Christ'. Although this *prima facie* appearance is then dismantled, Dante has nevertheless used such instances to trespass against certain settled assumptions and expectations of his readers. Despite the appearance of a seamless system, universal order is actually founded on exceptional grace, and the ultimate authority of God is precisely the authority to suspend the systematic rule of an inflexible regime based on calculable, iron laws. In the end, the system serves as an enabling structure for its own transcendence – and in this sense is destined to be 'transgressed'.

Accordingly, the *Comedy*, together with Dante's other writings, has served to support readings that portray him as an arch-transgressor and a revolutionary, as much as a reactionary intolerant of transgression in any form. The former view has been advocated most fervently by varied assortments of esoteric readers. Their ranks comprise the likes of Dante Gabriel Rossetti, Luigi Valli, Giovanni Pascoli, Eugène Aroux and René Guénon, who affiliate Dante with a number of heretical movements, from the Albigensians to the Joachimites, and with secret, mystical fraternities from the freemasons and Knights Templar to the *Fedeli d'Amore*.[3] Semi-novelistic versions of this heterodox Dante lend vivid colours to the image of the exiled poet as impenitent outlaw and sworn enemy of ecclesiastical authority and dogma.[4] There is no dearth of such inventions exploiting a free narrative vein in imagining Dante as an initiate, for example, of the secret order of the *Priorate di Sion* and as proffering an all-comprehensive esoteric *gnosis* in his poem aiming at the salvation of the world.

Portrayals of Dante as spiritual Franciscan or as Averroist similarly underline the transgressive features of his work and personality as viewed from various heterodox angulations.[5] And these are only some of the divergent directions which scholarship has taken in pursuit of the powerful sense of Dante's deep-seated disposition to transgressiveness, however it may be disguised. These currents prove relevant for assessing the role of transgression in Dante's life and work. Most importantly for our purposes, they invite us to take up the challenge of rethinking the very sense of transgression as we can rediscover it through reading Dante with acute alertness to our contemporary cultural context. I pursue this challenge in what follows by taking cues from provocative re-conceptualizations of transgression proposed especially by recent French theorists, signally Maurice Blanchot, Georges Bataille, Roland Barthes, Michel Foucault and Emmanuel Levinas.[6]

Sticking, however, for the moment to Dante's own writings, we cannot fail to observe that he insistently identifies with numerous exemplary and even archetypal figures of transgression. He feels close to – and at the same time is anxious to distance himself from – figures particularly of human artists transgressing upon divine prerogatives of creation. We sense this in the recurring references to Arachne (*Inf.* XVII.18; *Purg.* XII.43–5; *Par.* XVIII.64–6), who in her ill-considered bragging about her skill in the art of weaving offended the goddess Minerva and was metamorphosed into a spider. Likewise the miserable *Piche*, the nine daughters of King Pierus of Macedonia, who are turned into magpies as a result of their challenge to the nine Muses (Ovid, *Metamorphoses* V.294–678), are recalled by Dante at the outset of the *Purgatorio*, as he solicits the inspiration of the goddess Calliope (I.9-12), as if to remind himself not to overstep the bounds set for him as a mortal poet. Dante scholarship has documented the proliferating echoes of these allusions throughout the poem as obsessive and subtly insinuating motifs.[7]

Of the figures from the repertoire of Ovidian victims of the gods' vengeance against human artists who dared to rival them, it is the satyr Marsyas who is most tellingly compared to Dante himself. Carried away with pride over his performance on a flute (*tibia*) or reed (*harundo*) that had been cast away by Minerva because it creased her otherwise perfect features when she blew on it, he challenged Apollo to a music contest and, after losing, was flayed alive by the god (*Metamorphoses* VI.383-400). Marsyas is evoked at the outset of the *Paradiso* (I.20-1) as Dante prepares for yet higher flights of poetic song, relying still on his low instrument of the vernacular language, which is comparable to Marsyas's humble reed set against Apollo's golden lyre. By calling on the god Apollo to enter his breast and inspire him (*Entra nel petto mio, e spira tue*, I.19), just as he drew Marsyas out of his 'sheath' (in Italian the word is 'vagina', suggesting also a new birth), Dante aspires to shed his mortal skin and so casts himself as in some sense a sacrificial victim offered up for the sake of the poem, which he later dares to designate as 'sacred' (*poema sacro*, XXV.1).

The figures of Icarus and Phaethon also are associated with overambitious ventures into the heavens undertaken against their fathers' express warnings, and Dante is reminded of them when he feels himself stray all too near the danger of overstepping the natural limits for any normally earthbound voyager. He evokes them together in *Inferno* XVII.106-11, where flying on the back of Geryon, he clings closer to Virgil as his father elect, hoping to escape the temerarious sons' tragic fate. They become *exempla* of punishment for transgression against paternal authority, or at least for failure to heed sound paternal counsel. Even as he ascends towards his vision of God at the top of the heavens, Dante still thinks of Icarus, to such an extent that images of 'flight' or 'wings' are apt to connote this reference wherever they occur (*Par.* VIII.125-6; X.74; XV.54; XXXII.145-6).[8]

He contemplates how nearly he resembles these archetypes of transgressive overreaching of the usual human boundaries. His vision-quest places him in proximity and finally in direct contact with the divine and its humanly unendurable energy – like Semelè (*Par.* XXI.6) incinerated by the effulgence of Jove after she insisted (goaded by Juno) upon beholding openly the divine lover who visited her nightly, incognito.

The figures of metamorphosis abound in Dante's own text, particularly in the *Paradiso*. This is not least because his journey through Paradise is itself undeniably one of progressive metamorphoses, of radical changes – particularly in his powers of perception – with each new ascent through the successive heavens. In Paradise, he goes so far as to 'transhumanize' – to step beyond the threshold of the human and even beyond the furthest limits of saying: '*Trasumanar significar* per verba / *non si poria*' ('Transhumanizing cannot be signified in words', I.70–1). He is transformed and in some sense divinized, as he suggests emblematically by identifying with yet another mythic personality, the figure of Glaucus. Glaucus became a sea god (*consorto in mar de li altri dèi, Par.* I.69) through ingestion of the herb that he had observed had power to reanimate the fish he caught and laid down dead upon it (*Metamorphoses* XIII.904–68).

Beyond these Ovidian mythological contents and their transgressive connotations, there is another level at which the overstepping of limits is at work in Dante's text: the neologism 'trasumanar' exemplifies Dante's constant recourse to invention of an unprecedented new language. His language persistently exceeds the signs that are available to him in the currency of the Italian language he inherits.[9] He explores the vocabulary of transcendence through a plethora of transumptive verbs such as 'trasmodar', 'trasmutar', 'trapassar', 'traslatar'. Dante is surpassing all precedents and transgressing all limits that are normally binding for human poets and their prowess. His course dangerously parallels Ulysses's venturing beyond the columns set by Hercules at the outer boundary of the navigable world. By such allusions, the theme of transgression is woven in filigree into Dante's *magnum opus*.

Particularly the *Paradiso*, with its quest to see God directly and to unite with the divine essence – a quest fused with the project of going beyond all previous human endeavours in poetry – is full of the danger of transgression of human limits and of trespass upon the holy. The danger of failing to heed the incomparable superiority and transcendence of the divine is kept at bay only by constant acknowledgement and by persistent self-humbling prostrations.

Accordingly, the examples evoked especially from Ovid are generally ones from which Dante *dis*sociates himself in the end.[10] They are *exempla* warning against the temptation to venture out beyond the parameters sanctioned for human endeavour. However, unlike their endeavours, Dante's journey, for all its astonishing boldness, is authorized from above and is therefore *not* transgressive, not anyway of the supreme authority governing the universe, namely, God's. Dante places himself circumspectly within the bounds of the mission that has been assigned to him by the heavenly powers. When he doubts whether his own journey to the other world is perhaps illegitimate and presumptuous, Virgil lays these doubts to rest by telling of how he himself was called upon by heaven to come and rescue Dante wandering lost in the dark wood. Similarly, in Dante's own case, as writer no less than as voyager, none of his rash and racy originality counts as transgressive, at least not by his own accounting. He sets himself up as the instrument and vehicle – rather than as the rival or challenger – of divinity. He prays to Apollo to make him a worthy vessel (*sì fatto vaso, Par.* I.14). The wording here of 'chosen vessel' hints that he is closer to Saint Paul, the *vas electionis* of Acts 9:15, already evoked as *vas d'elezione* in *Inferno* II.28, than to the Ovidian characters who are condemned to perish by their inordinate hubris.

Indeed Dante is guided all along the way by God's emissaries and mediators. This is a crucial sign of his difference from the transgressors, to whom he often feels himself to be perilously close. When at the outset he hesitates to embark on the journey, lest it be a 'mad' undertaking (*temo che la venuta non sia folle, Inf.* II.35), he anticipates the phrase 'mad flight' (*folle volo, Inf.* XXVI.125) that encapsulates Ulysses's uninvited and fatal venture. The comparison with Ulysses in the end serves to underscore how Dante's own case is fundamentally different, given the backing of the divine summons relayed by three blessed ladies that he receives through Virgil, his guide.

Nonetheless, in spite of all these reassurances, it is evident that Dante's worries are not laid to rest. The 'mad crossing of Ulysses' (*il varco folle di Ulisse, Par.* XXVII.82–3) is recalled yet again in Dante's last look back at the earth from the heavenly spheres, just as he passes beyond the planetary and stellar universe into the *Primo Mobile*, the border of the physical universe, beyond which he is no longer in space and time. And again, Adam's sin is referred to by Beatrice similarly as 'follía' (*madness*), in her explanation of the doctrine of the atonement in *Paradiso* VII.93. In this manner, the motif of Ulysses's 'mad flight' is woven together linguistically with the paradigm of the original human sin. Such language makes it plain that archetypal sin is folly specifically in the sense of transgression – of going beyond the limits prescribed by authority, ultimately God's. Adam, chafing against the limits set for his own ambition, falls into sin 'for not suffering the virtue that wished to bridle his prowess' (*per non soffrire a la virtù che vole / freno a suo prode, Par.* VII.25–7).

In general, starting from the Adamic archetype, Dante figures sin as a matter of prideful, self-willed overstepping of boundaries. Too daring or arduous a striving on the basis of one's own mad desire, as opposed to minding authority and the limits it sets, leads humans astray and into perdition. *Ardito* belongs to the same semantic web as *folle*, with which it is interwoven in *Inferno* VIII.90–1: the furies enjoin Dante to return alone, without Virgil, along the *folle strada* – the 'mad road' – which has brought him to the Gate of Dis, after his 'rash' (*ardito*) entry into Hell alive. The final description of Adam's sin in *Paradiso* XXXII redeploys this adjective in recalling the tasting of the forbidden fruit as *l'ardito gusto. Paradiso* XXIX.52–7, furthermore, identifies the cause of the fall of the angels as the pride or 'superbir' – etymologically perhaps a superb or arrogant 'going beyond' (*super-b-ire*) – of Satan, in contrast with the 'modesty' of the good angels, who recognized themselves as created by the divine Goodness. Such offshoots of the semantics of transgression ramify all through Dante's poem.

Of course, Dante's own movements as represented in the poem lead him back always to God, in unhesitating obedience to his Creator: they are thus portrayed as diametrically contrary to any will to transgression. And yet how strong his sense of identification with the transgressors he reprimands! How torn he feels over any demand to reign in or renounce his quest! Does he not always find a way to pursue his adventure, nonetheless, without relinquishing its most alluring possibilities or forgoing any of its most arduous challenges? Unsurprisingly, therefore, he continues to be haunted by the figure of Ulysses. In spite of all his pious intentions, Dante cannot elude his destiny to become recognized, in crucial respects, as the first modern European individual, remaking the world through his own irrepressible passion and imagination. He counts, in this regard, as a precursor on the path leading eventually to Faust and the Romantic Overreacher.[11]

As appears already from this initial inventory, the nodal points of greatest relief, most sharply pinpointing the theme of transgression in the *Divine Comedy*, are Ulysses's journey beyond the Pillars of Hercules and Adam's trespass against the commandment of God in Eden. The episodes are related in the twenty-sixth cantos of the *Inferno* and of the *Paradiso*, respectively, thereby staking out an itinerary of the theme of transgression that spans the architecture of the *Comedy* as a whole.[12] Moreover, the one episode recalls the other, since they are linked in the semantic texture of the poem by forms of the word 'sign' used both in *Inferno* XXVI (*dov'Ercule segnò i suoi riguardi*, 108) and in *Paradiso* XXVI (*il trapassar del segno*, 117).

All human sin, Dante suggests, can be comprehended generically as in some way a repetition of the original, archetypal trespassing of the sign by Adam. The paramount importance of this sin, in being the first, could not be made plainer. Nevertheless, Ulysses's case seems to Dante to come nearest to his own, as is betrayed by the poet's continuing rumination of the Ulysses's motif and by the protagonist's visceral empathy with this character, towards whom his 'desire' instinctively bends (*vedi che del disio ver' lei mi piego!, Inf.* XXVI.69). In Ulysses's presence, even Dante the writer feels himself admonished to reign in his own 'genius'.

Hercules's Pillars, which Ulysses passes beyond, are signs meant to circumscribe all human voyages 'so that no man should venture further' (*acciò che l'uom più oltre non si metta, Inf.* XXVI.109). And similarly Adam's original sin is understood as a transgression of the limits set by God for human beings. In reply to Dante's mental question concerning the reason for God's great disdain in the Garden, Adam says that his sin was not tasting the forbidden fruit but only his transgressing the limit set – his 'trespass of the sign' (*solamente il trapassar del segno, Par.* XXVI.117) – in disobeying the divine injunction not to eat of the fruit from the tree of knowledge of good and evil.

That transgression in these lapidary formulations should figure as a trespassing of the *sign* is a verbal hint that invites concentrated reflection. Dante's *Paradiso* enacts a transgression and even a 'deconstruction' of the sign in a journey beyond the limits of language – beyond the ability of signs to signify – that calls to be elaborated in terms of semiotic theory. I pursue one possible approach to this task in the ensuing chapters. In this introductory chapter, I have begun by summarily inventorying the chief emblems of transgression that stud Dante's poem and show how transgression turns out to be a most provocative theme. It emerges in crucial respects as the central issue in Dante's overall vision of human history and destiny.

Dante's repertoire of transgressive figures includes also Nimrod (*Inf.* XXXI.67–81; *Purg.* XII.35), who is emblematic of the fall of humankind as entailing specifically and indeed eminently the fall of language. By building the tower of Babel, the giant transgressed the created division of heaven from earth and induced humans by their 'art' to transgress upon (*superare*) nature and its Maker.[13] Also the unprecedented voyage of Jason and the Argonauts, which was traditionally the first sea voyage and presumably an illicit trespassing on the sea god's previously inviolate precincts, frames the *Paradiso* by allusions in II.16–18 and XXXIII.94–6. It belongs to the dense web of classical references that subtend the question of transgression raised by Dante's journey to the other world. We will consider its relevance specifically to the transgression of the sign in due course.

Crucial among the Scriptural allusions bearing on this issue is also Dante's comparison of himself to Saint Paul at the moment of the latter's *raptus* to the third or highest heaven. This ecstatic moment is recalled in the opening lines of the *Paradiso* (I.6, 73–5), with its echoes of II Corinthians 12:4 concerning Paul's having heard 'inexpressible words, which it is not lawful for a man to utter' (*arcana verba, quae non licet homini loqui*). This comparison is audacious to the point of collapsing the partition between the sacred and the profane. And yet Dante in his poem, unlike Paul in his epistle, refuses to renounce the desire to tell of his experience of Paradise. Dante risks trespassing upon the border that separates divinity from humanity, and the nature of this risk comes to focus as specifically linguistic. What for Paul are ineffable words (*arrheta rhemata*), Dante strives to utter. Though they be transgressive and unlawful for a man to say, that does not stop Dante from trying!

Having first highlighted the motif of transgression *within* Dante's poem, we will be chiefly concerned in what follows with the poem itself as an instance of transgression – the most crucial one. We noted that Dante's art in the *Paradiso* is supremely an art of 'transhumanization' (I.70). His poem makes a claim to being not merely human but divine – a 'sacro poema', one to which human and divine authors have lent their hands respectively (*Par.* XXV.2). One motive for the pervasive sense of transgression in Dante's poem – especially when viewed from our post-Romantic perspective – is certainly its asserting the remarkable, if not miraculous, power of poetry to intervene upon the world and to change it. As such, Dante's poem has the potential to play a prophetic and even a messianic role. For modern readers, Dante's work may be only an artistic creation. Nevertheless, this invention radically questions the limits of art and its borders with reality. In this respect, the underlying 'sense' of transgression, deeper than any explicit theme, is a sense that Dante might perhaps be usurping God's prerogative in creation – like the Ovidian characters who challenged the gods' superiority in various genres of artistic creation and were punished for it.

Dante's audacity and his poem's unprecedented ambitions as a creative work far outdo those of even Ovid's most immodest offenders. Dante does not directly claim to be remaking the world but only to be making a poem. Yet he allows us to begin to sense how such a poeticological creative act could be an original invention and, in some sense, a substantial remaking of reality. This sense was destined to become much more conscious and acute as poetry progressed into the modern age, especially in its Romantic phase. Hence Dante's status as inaugural author of modernity – as has been explored often and from varying angles.[14] However, the project I pursue here springs from substantially different motivations and matrices. What are now often called 'postmodern' perspectives permit us to glimpse a yet further degree of transgressiveness in Dante's language that goes beyond the demiurgic forging of reality (especially by a re-narrating of history) and beyond signification altogether. Following indicators of this 'beyond' (Dante's *trans*), we will explore how Dante's work embodies an even more provocative sense of transgression.

We will simultaneously discover how transgression is being rethought in our own time as not necessarily, and in any case not simply, a going against established law or order. French postmodern thinkers have reconceived 'transgression' at its most original and disturbing as not oppositional at all. Transgression in the traditional sense inevitably recognizes and even tends to reaffirm the order it opposes. Transgressors publicly punished – or at least condemned – in the name of the law, actually confirm and reinforce it. The deepest and most dangerous – but perhaps also most messianic or saving – type of transgression is of a different order altogether. It renders ineffective the binary principles enabling distinction between transgressors and non-transgressors – those supposedly in good standing and those falling foul of a general system of governance. Transgression in this sense upsets the very possibility of decidable exclusions.

Paradoxically, the contemporary thinking of 'difference' pushes to this limit and undermines all exclusionary distinctions between inside and outside, thereby restoring an original openness and connectedness of all with all. This is what is at stake ultimately in the 'negative theology' that informs mystical experience. Negative theology maintains simply that we can know only what God is *not*, and mystics of various sorts have lived accordingly in unconditional openness to what they do not and cannot know, excluding nothing. Such a perspective can be seen as inherent in Christianity or, more exactly, in the Christ event as embodying just such a radical transgressivity in the complete giving up of self. Dante's *Paradiso*, moreover, demonstrates this subversion of the very oppositional logic of language in exemplary fashion. This involves negative or equivalently 'apophatic' theology ('apophasis' being Greek for 'negation') in a tradition stemming from Dionysius the Areopagite (fifth–sixth century A.D.) that Dante knew well.[15] Its affinities with postmodern styles of especially French criticism are brought out as peculiarly revealing in the analysis that ensues. These theoretical stakes are worked out in Part One in terms of poetic language as an experience of the unsayable, following Blanchot and Barthes on the non-oppositional logic of what they both call the 'neuter'.

This theoretical transposing of the issue of transgression, however, will serve not to definitively abandon the more concrete questions of Dante's social, political and ecclesiological trangressiveness but rather to prepare us for a return, equipped with certain more subtle means of discernment, to these issues in Part Two. There, Dante's poetic use of the language of theology as a revelation of divinity incarnate in human life and eminently in the institutions of the Papacy and the Empire is treated in its capacity for undermining all partisan power. The theoretical consequences of the argument are then drawn out in terms of inner experience (as understood by Bataille and Blanchot) and transcendence (in the sense of Levinas) in Part Three. This itinerary will engender insight into why simple alignment with or against authority cannot be Dante's position. There are reasons why Dante must appear to be both minding and undermining, both bolstering and bucking, the institutional authorities that he in one way or another is bound to confront and transgress.

Finally an 'Appendix' is offered as a microcosm of the book in the sense of being its original cell. I first developed this theoretical approach to Dante's paradisiacal poetics through engagement with Levinas's philosophy, itself the seed of so much of Blanchot's (not to mention Derrida's) most transgressive thinking. This constellation of connections between mystical theology, French deconstruction and poetics has been approached previously with distinction particularly by Kevin Hart in various works cited from the very subtitle of the present book (where Hart's own title is restored to its source in Dante). Hart's sense of the poetics of apophaticism, of the possibilities for literary expression that open up in the wake of negative theology (with its check to proper, predicative expression concerning God and consequently concerning everything else too), is an inspiration for contributions to the field of religion and literature, such as is attempted in these pages.

Part One

Language and Beyond

2

The Linguistic Turn of Transgression in the *Paradiso*

Beyond all the suggestive emblems that hint at an obsession with transgression beneath Dante's overt suppression of it, there is another and a prior sense in which transgression emerges as Dante's essential and ultimate gesture, his final testament. His work as a poet culminates in the *Paradiso* with a transcendence of language towards the purely ineffable, mystical experience of heavenly paradise – the Empyrean – and ultimately of the theological mysteries of the Holy Trinity and the Incarnate Son. This involves a transcendence of language to a realm purportedly beyond language. Yet Dante conveys the experience, nevertheless, in and through language and specifically through the *transgression* of language, inasmuch as such expression requires a violation of the normal function of the sign. He employs language in the *Paradiso* in ways that surpass its referential use and turn it intensively in the direction of self-reference or of direct self-manifestation. Such language transgresses against what a number of medieval authorities who could hardly be ignored considered to be the proper function of language.[1] In particular, the linguistic theory of Saint Augustine, especially as articulated in *De Doctrina Christiana*, authoritatively established the referring of signs (*signa*) to things (*res*) as the basis of the meaningfulness and legitimacy of language.[2]

We should not, however, overlook Augustine's own 'trespassing, eluding and superseding the strictures of linguistic thought', inasmuch as he mixes his semiotics with theology.[3] He makes the universe itself a system of signs pointing to its Creator, and to this extent, he already collapses the sign-thing distinction. While the order of being is in principle distinct from and independent of the order of signifying,

Augustine in fact acknowledges that signs are things in defining them as 'things that signify other things', while conversely he admits that things are also signs, in discerning a symbolic and indeed a teleological order to the universe in which everything turns out to be significant. To this extent, the transgression of the sign can be seen to be written implicitly into its definition in this Christian transcription, which thus already harbours the sign's own self-deconstruction.

Dante's *Paradiso*, as a whole, by virtue of its most original and characteristic mode of signifying, communicates fundamentally through a transgression of the sign: where the sign fails, collapses and explodes – that is the point where the type of significance most proper and peculiar to the *Paradiso* is manifestly realized. Semiologically considered, it is not by anything that language can properly say via the regular application of its grammatical forms and by normal employment of its semantic material, but only by transgressing the proper use of these linguistic means, that the *Paradiso* delivers its peculiarly uncanny message and attains to the divine vision. The *Paradiso* does consist all throughout in exact statements with perfectly definite doctrinal sense, yet at the same time it constantly denies that anything it says can be adequate to its true meaning. It is through *un*saying what it says that this far more important *unsayable* meaning – or perhaps rather transgression of meaning and suspension of sense – is achieved. In this respect, the *Paradiso* borrows from traditions of negative theology which were familiar to Dante through the works of philosopher-theologians such as Augustine and Dionysius the Areopagite and many others throughout medieval tradition up to Thomas Aquinas and even to Dante's own contemporaries, particularly Meister Eckhart.[4] Dante ingeniously adapts to poetry the negative theological outlook of these religious thinkers and poetically exploits the closely associated techniques of apophatic mysticism.

Criticism has often recognized that Dante's language takes a pronounced mystical turn in the *Paradiso*. It is a chief theme of a number of books on the language of the *Paradiso*.[5] There is, moreover, a pronounced transgressiveness inherent in such language. The mystical word in general is frequently and not inaccurately characterized as being 'of great verbal impertinence and of great linguistic transgressiveness' (*di grande impertinenza verbale, di grande trasgressività linguistica*).[6]

Yet Dante's *Divine Comedy* is often taken in general cultural currency (more than in specialized scholarly literature) to represent the establishment of a total semiotic system – and along with it a whole political-moral-historical order of the world – on unshakeable foundations, lending all a solid anchorage in the heavens. Dante presumably affirms a metaphysical doctrine that refers all that exists to an eternal, divine Presence. He thereby would also ground all signs in the ultimate transcendental Signified, namely, God, giving them stable and in principle unambiguous significance. This view stands behind Kevin Hart's summary, in *The Trespass of the Sign*, of the 'unmistakable' significance of Dante's major work:

> Dante's point in the *Commedia* is unmistakable: the proliferation of signs caused by Adam and increased by those such as Master Adam can be arrested only by a belief that Christ, the New Adam, is the faithful sign of God. Without the presence of God, in Paradise or on earth, there can be no hope of understanding oneself, others, or texts. One would be lost in a maze of sins, with no possibility of distinguishing true from false.[7]

Hart states that secure grounding of signs would not be possible, according to Dante, without the divine presence in heaven and even on earth in incarnate form in Christ. The inference is that the divine presence, then, does provide precisely this guarantee of the true value of signs. Now Dante may perhaps lend himself to being cast as representing what is, at least before being tainted by sin, a closed universe staked out by certifiable truths entrusted to stable signs. The stability and transparency of these signs can be lost or obscured, but their meaning is in principle ascertainable and assured by God's unfailing presence. Such a universe is often presumed to be envisaged by a typically medieval worldview and may be deemed to have been credible only before the eruptions and explorations that unsettled this symbolic order and ushered in the modern age, the so-called age of discovery, with its empty, unbounded space.

Yet, beyond the constraints of such a perfunctory role as pillar of medieval tradition, Dante's poem is even more concerned with the realization of the dynamism of language. Dante's choice of language is the first unmistakably revolutionary aspect of his literary enterprise: he commits his poem to the vernacular – to a historically evolving medium of communication – as opposed to the fixed, grammatical language of Latin. Even if the *Commedia* is about building a linguistic-symbolic system that can comprehend all of reality in a unified vision and as a stable metaphysical and moral order, its final movement, the *Paradiso*, is also just as much about *un*doing anything such as a fixed system – even as the sun 'unseals' the snow that is melted by its heat, or just as Sibyl's leaves bearing the divine oracles are scattered to the winds (*Par.* XXXIII.64–6). The order of eternity turns out to be open and elusive and full of unforeseeable surprises.

As intimated by the metaphors or figures employed for Dante's final vision in the Empyrean, as well as in its preliminary versions all through the ascent across the nine physical heavens, the vision explodes in a shattering and scattering of its words and letters and finally in a forgetting (*letargo*) of signs altogether. They are represented eminently as sparks and seeds – as processes of spontaneous combustion and dissemination – all through the *Paradiso*. Such are the images that filter across the canticle in order to reveal the total dynamism of an always new language, the creative language of poetic invention that transgresses every prior canon and every reigning discursive convention that would fix and prescribe the form of speech by an authoritative norm.

Certainly, language in Dante's Christian theological perspective is underwritten in the end by the divine Word incarnate, but not as if this necessarily established stable, immutable significance that could be fixed in the terms of a standing linguistic order. It is rather the dissolving of all finite significance in the Infinite that gives words their ultimate theological authority – or, better, authenticity – as well as their poetic significance – or rather *ultra*-significance – in the self-subverting play of language under erasure in the *Paradiso*. It is as a phenomenon of vanishing that language achieves its meaning in Dante's last poem – which paradoxically becomes so lasting!

This can be seen most perspicuously in the *visibile parlare* (visible speech) of the astonishing spectacle of sky-writing that Dante views in the Heaven of Jove – the 'jovial' (*giovïal*) heaven (*Par.* XVIII.70), as a pun in the first line of its description significantly suggests. Thirty-five letters appear successively in the firmament. Together they spell a sentence of Scripture, the *incipit* of the Book of Wisdom: *DILigite Iustitiam Qui Iudicatis Terram* ('Love justice you who rule the earth'). The letters appear one by one, and each one is presented as a visible spectacle in its own right. Each is contemplated by Dante as a direct manifestation of God, and each lends itself to being interpreted as representing one of the Divine Names: 'D' for *Dio* in Italian (or *Deo* in Latin), 'I' for the original Name of God in human language as spoken first by Adam, as we learn later in XXVI.134, and 'L' for *EL*, the name of God in Hebrew. Each of these three initial letters, which are highlighted by the text, being set off from the rest of the sentence, can be decrypted as a Name of God. Beyond these specific cases, all letters could be considered as Divine Names and in fact were so contemplated in the Kabbalah. But the first three letters of the sentence seem to be highlighted in order to make this possibility more conspicuously evident. So understood, each of the letters painted in the heaven is a foretaste of the vision of divinity towards which the whole poem yearns. In the form of these letters, Dante immediately *sees* the Word of God. He experiences the presence of God in letters drawn directly from the Bible.

The vision of writing in this heaven suggests that the vision of God can be approached, if at all, only through a vision in and even *of* language. What Dante sees are the words and, even more reductively, the letters of Scripture. His vision is of language and specifically of writing seen in its constitutive components – letters. This immediate vision of the medium of his poem, namely, writing, conveys the idea of immediacy of vision. By taking its own medium as the metaphor of immediacy, Dante's text is hinting that the immediacy of vision which should in principle characterize the vision of God is paradoxically a vision in and through writing – the medium of mediation par excellence.[8] Mediation (writing) becomes the metaphor for immediacy (vision).[9]

To follow the implications of this a step further, it is more precisely in the dissolution of language that the *Paradiso*'s vision of God is achieved. For the letters are shown to be composed of soul-sparks shooting to and fro. Far from being a stable form, each letter is formed by unpredictable eruptions and combustion of component sparks that break up after an instant in order to re-form moments later into other shapes. The whole order of grammar (vowel and consonant, noun and verb) is here made to rest on apparently random chance.

Accordingly, God is 'seen' not as a discrete object like a letter but rather in the differential play of signifiers that generates significance and creates linguistic meaning. Conceived thus, language consists not in static forms but rather in the ceaselessly circulating mutual references and reciprocal determinations of interdependent signs and signifiers. This infinite mediation is more essentially language's immediate substance than any graphic or phonic form in which it materially takes on shape or sound in external space and in perceived time. The miracle is that such apparently random shooting of marks, like a sparking of material particles, should turn out, after all, to mean something.

In the heaven of Jove, the helter-skelter chaos of sparking (*sfavillar*) miraculously forms a speaking (*favella*), the way birds on the wing, especially when migrating, organize themselves into formations resembling letters. They do so irrationally through an instinct which is implanted in them by a higher guide than reason – by nature's own divine Creator (*Quei che dipinge lì*, XVIII.109–11). Conceived in this manner, the intelligibility of writing emerges from beyond any rational intention or control on the part of creatures. It is a miraculous manifestation of divine Presence, even if in the form of writing, and thus in the medium of absence, given the radical separation between sign and referent, between signifier and meaning, that is inherent in the written sign.

All the apparently random chaos of history likewise turns out to be providentially guided by God (*esso guida*, 110). Dante is given to understand this from his vision in this heaven, where language is dissolved into haphazardly shooting particles of its perceptible substrate – in this case, the flashes of souls serving as graphic marks. Language is broken down in this way into component parts that cannot be commanded by any graspable law of matter in motion or of intelligible composition. Yet God is present here in the divine meaning that emerges from what otherwise appears to be chaos. The final letter M of the phrase that has formed from the sparks then explodes, as when a firebrand is struck (*come nel percuoter di ciocchi arsi*, XVIII.100), and the innumerable randomly emitted sparks (*surgono innumerevoli faville*, 101) miraculously form into the head and neck of an eagle – the emblem of Empire through which justice is to be providentially established on earth. Only such apparent chaos can reveal a mystical meaning beyond the grasp of human reason: any rationally intelligible principle would fall short of the transcendent sense that Dante envisages in the *Paradiso*.

The transcendence of sense, specifically the miraculous vindication of justice that Dante sees written in the heaven of Jupiter, is made manifest by an effect of language decomposed into the parts of speech (*parti*) arrayed in binary oppositions between vowel and consonant, noun and verb. Five times seven letters (= 35, the number of years attained by Christ's life on earth, according to *Convivio* IV.xxiii.10) form the words of the first sentence of the book of Wisdom – and then are further decomposed into a swarm of luminous sparks.

The exuberant display seems to be totally irrational, yet the sense of a *speaking* is found, as if by dint of a miracle, in this play of differences formed by a chaos of *sparking*. Sparking turns graphically into speaking: *sfavillar* (sparking) is revealed as *favellar* (speaking). Through the juxtaposition of these sonorously similar, indeed nearly identical, words, phonetics itself suggests that meaningful speaking is produced by the apparently mindless sparking of particles that resolve themselves into significant patterns of words and sentences. What appears miraculously to Dante's eyes lets him understand that the apparent chaos he observes on earth is actually an effect of divine justice.

Semiotically considered, Dante's *Paradiso* depicts the deconstruction of language as a system of signs. The graphic marks of the poem become sparks communicating an immediate energy and revealing a meaning more intuitive and visionary than all that can be grasped through the discursive mechanism of sign and referent. Language as such breaks down on Dante's journey to the Unsayable – to the beyond of language as based on signs functioning referentially in relation to the world. Dante's poem seeks to realize and indeed surpass the ultimate possibilities of language. The spectacle of writing in Jove transcends linguistic signification and conveys or intimates sense in a more direct and palpable way – by an incandescent, iridescent, visionary speaking/sparking: a sparkling display of speech, if ever there was one.

It is not simply by abandoning language but rather through a transgression of language's normal rules, in such a way as imposes language all the more directly and immanently, that this transcendence of language is achieved by Dante's poem. It is *within and by means of language* that he transcends its furthest capacities and limits and so takes the 'step beyond' – the '*pas au-delà*', in the peculiarly suggestive and self-contradictory vocabulary of Maurice Blanchot (see Chapter 4 below).

Addendum on self-referentiality and transcendence

The self-referentiality of language, particularly poetic language, which is conspicuously constituted by self-reflexive patterns of rhythm and rhyme, assonance and anaphora, might seem to be a structure of self-enclosure and of monotonous repetition of the same. It can seem to represent a failure of language in its chief task, namely, to refer and communicate. Yet, in Dante's theological vision, such self-reflexivity of poetic language is not vitiated by Narcissistic self-enclosure: it rather opens into an imitation of the creative source of all being, namely, transcendent divinity in its self-reflexive Trinitarian structure. This inner being of God is inexhaustibly fecund in its creative activity throughout the universe, and it is mirrored by language in its limitless production of proliferating significances. Dante's poetry aims to evoke and even to materially realize the divine vision of the inner life of divinity in the structure and dynamics of language itself: language in this sense becomes the object or manifestation of the divine vision for which it also serves as medium.

This self-reflexive function of poetic language is Narcissistic, as the poem's imagery subtly admits, but it constitutes a redeemed Narcissism.[10] The self-reflection of the celestial Rose, as in a limpid, aqueous surface, is the culmination of the programme of references to Narcissus in the 30th cantos of each of the canticles. Damnation to licking the mirror of Narcissus in *Inferno* XXX.127–9 and the penitential self-mirroring of the sinner in *Purgatorio* XXX.76–8 metamorphose in *Paradiso* XXX.109–15 into a glorious mirroring of divinity throughout creation. Especially the blessed souls in Paradise are likenesses to God himself. The motif of self-reflection and self-referentiality persists all the way to the end of the poem. It is, in effect, present and evidenced in every poetic word, each itself a miniature engine of self-reflection.

The self-referentiality of poetic language is for Dante at the same time a reference to transcendence, the transcendence of divinity as revealed in the Christian religion. The archetype of self-referentiality is the Trinitarian God, supreme in its transcendence of all creation and even of Being itself, according to the negative theology of Dionysius the Areopagite. This theology lies at the root of a mystical tradition leading to Bernard and Bonaventure, which is in many ways integrated into the theological underpinnings of the *Paradiso*. Whereas self-referentiality has typically been seen as Narcissistic and has often been condemned in medieval and also in postmodern thought as a futile form of self-enclosure, for Dante self-referentiality reveals the sacred nature of God the Father perfectly reflected in his only begotten Son and one with the Holy Spirit as a further reflection outward of their intimate, indivisible oneness. Self-reflection thus modelled by the Trinity is not sterile and closed in on itself but rather the creative reproduction and giving of self propagated infinitely outward into the world. Self-reflexivity for Dante, particularly the self-reflectiveness of poetic language wrought to its uttermost in the *Paradiso*, is itself a reflection of such theological transcendence. Far from remaining imprisoned in immanence, it becomes a reflection of divinity and of its creativity *ad extra*.

3

At the Limits of Language or Reading Dante through Blanchot

'Transgression', from the Latin *trans*, across, and *gradior*, to step or walk (*gressus*: step), means, etymologically, 'stepping across'. In the *Paradiso*, Dante steps across the boundaries of language into the realm of the unsayable. In this literal sense, he is a transgressor in his literary acts as writer all through the poem considered as a rhetorical performance. This predicament is mirrored diegetically in the transgressiveness of an extraterrestrial journey by a terrestrial being that the poem recounts. Dante maps his progress, both as protagonist and as poet, as a series of thresholds that he steps across. At the same time, he shows the impossibility of transgression, or how each stepping beyond remains within a sphere of immanence and fails to attain objectively the transcendent reality towards which and by which his every step is directed. His ultimate aim is the vision of God, but this goal, though it motivates him at every turn, proves nonetheless to be an 'impossibility'. It is precisely *as* impossible that Dante imagines it to have actually taken place – and then only through a miracle of divine grace.

Even if we grant that on the journey itself Dante somehow finally transcends the created sphere and crosses the abyss to the Creator, nevertheless in his literary quest, he remains – as long as he speaks – always within a sphere of immanence to language. Accordingly, Dante's persistent, underlying theme in the *Paradiso* becomes his failure to be able to express his experience. For it is not enough simply to *say* that he saw God, he wants to make it actually happen – in language – by the 'making' of *poiesis*. For this purpose, he needs to make his medium transcendent even in its immanence.

Dante's human task of realizing and conveying his vision in the end turns out to consist in reproducing its humanly insurmountable difficulty. The vision in some sense coincides with presenting the full force of the *experience of its impossibility*. The poem constantly presents excuses for not being able to convey the essential vision on which it is purportedly based – and thereby evokes and presents it, after all, in the only way it can. The poem presents its vision in language – a self-subverting, self-annulling, transgressive language. Paradise is, to this extent, the *Paradiso*. The divine vision is, in this sense, more precisely a non-vision: it is rather the absolute experience of language.

God himself cannot be seen. This is a principle for which Dante has Scriptural authority: 'No man hath ever seen God' (John 1:18). The spatio-temporal universe that *can* be seen in all the intricate interconnectedness of everything that is (substances and accidents) is a sign of the God that cannot as such be seen. Dante's vision is displaced from God himself to the whole book of the universe – which comprises all substances and accidents tied together by love (*legato con amore in un volume, / ciò che per l'universo si squaderna:/sustanze e accidenti*, XXXIII.85–8). The impossible vision of God is the enabling condition of this vision of All in lieu of God Himself according to his own proper essence (*in se*). But in the *Paradiso*, it is even more directly in language that the invisible God becomes manifest to Dante. More essentially than as reference to things that are seen, language is revealed here as indirect manifestation of the *un*seen.

There can be no visible object for the vision of God that is envisioned by the poem. God is not an object. Rather, the intransitive reality of language in its absoluteness becomes a kind of manifestation of the invisible and absolute. The *Paradiso*'s language does not so much report actual 'vision' – God cannot be 'seen' – as become itself a visionary manifestation of absolute reality. Thus, Dante's God is approached by relinquishing every name and moving outside of every positive field of representation in which objects can be seen or grasped. This is what Blanchot calls the Outside, and it is reached (or rather not reached) by a step/not beyond (*pas au-delà*).

Both Dante and Blanchot explore language to its limits in order to discover the radical Other to language and so open language up to its Outside. Both discover what transcends language through pursuing to its limit the experience of remaining essentially immanent to language. For Blanchot, this Outside is 'infinite', but Blanchot does not want to divinize the infinite or to find 'God' in the experience of infinite openness, as Dante does. For Dante, on the other hand, God is essentially Word. Yet this Word is in the end the transcendent Word of negative theology that no human words can remotely attain – except through subverting themselves and opening to their Outside.

Blanchot observes that writing, in the purest sense, when it is not made to serve any extrinsic purpose, when it 'seems devoted to nothing but itself' (*semble ne se consacrer qu'à elle-même*)[1] – what Roman Jakobson described as the 'poetic function' of language – paradoxically opens ways of being in relation to all, all that it places in question. In an 'anonymous, distracted, deferred and dispersed manner, writing frees up possibilities of being in relation to all because it places all into question, starting from the idea of God, the I, the Subject and then Truth and the One ...' (*Écrire ... dégage des possibilités toutes autres, une façon anonyme, distraite, différée et dispersée d'être en rapport par laquelle tout est mis en cause, et d'abord l'idée de Dieu, du Moi, du Sujet, puis de la Vérité et de l'Un* ... ibid.).

Writing, in this sense, for Blanchot, is 'the greatest violence because it transgresses the Law, every law and its own law' (*Écrire, sous ce point de vue, est la violence la plus grande, car elle transgresse la Loi, toute loi et sa propre loi*, p. viii). Writing, as creative, remakes the world and leaves nothing untouched or standing in place: in order to create, writing destroys the world. The whole universe in relation to writing, which creates an order or disorder all its own, is open to question and exploration and is not confined by any independently established laws. This transgressive relation to All is a manner of relating that will prove uncannily appropriate for construing also Dante's construction of the universe in relation to the transcendent, unattainable 'ground' of All. This ground is a God who ultimately cannot be represented, one whom

Dante approaches through the vehicle of his writing, which becomes a journey to God in its own right.

One can, of course, find a Hegelian type of project in Dante – a perfect synthesis of the whole of the real in a form of 'absolute knowing'. The total synthesis of reality in Dante's poem is what has for a long time most impressed many even of his most astute readers.[2] Hegel's thinking, moreover, is profoundly incarnational and thinks through to a historical conclusion the incarnational aspect of Christian revelation that is crucial also for Dante's vision. However, whereas Hegel's incarnate transcendence is pure identity with a fully articulated immanence, Dante in the end, in the poetry of the *Paradiso*, speaks through the breaches of his discursive system in order to summon up the Outside of the poem as a transcendence that is not articulated by the poem – not even as 'Transcendence', any more than as immanence. It is not grasped at all by the language of the poem but is allowed to approach as what the poem cannot as such signify. Such is at least one sense of Dante's insistence on the ineffability topos from the beginning to the end of the *Paradiso*.

Hegel attempts to provide a totally articulated system of reality as a whole, and certainly Dante undertakes a similar project, yet he interrupts it and consigns the totality in question to a God beyond his grasp, one to whom he relates in silence and in the breakdown of his own merely human speech. He constantly interrupts his narrative (*desisto*) and jumps outside of the corner into which he has inevitably written himself (*salta la penna*). Yet it is still the pen that jumps, and to this extent his jump outside discourse remains immanent to it. This is the movement of non/transcendence that calls to be read alongside the experience of writing described by Blanchot as the step/not beyond. Of course, Dante is a poet of transcendence, but he also transcends abstract transcendence and the simple opposition between transcendence and immanence. We need to try to understand the step beyond oppositional logic that he takes in the course of his translation of theological concepts into poetic experience. This is where especially Blanchot's thought on the limit-experience of literature can assist us.

At the Limits of Language or Reading Dante through Blanchot   33

My goal here is not to furnish a historical understanding of Dante's idea of language and the sources from which his concepts derive, but rather to pursue the speculative challenge represented by Dante's vision. Especially in the *Paradiso*, Dante is dealing with fascinating virtual and liminal aspects of language that have been approached similarly and differently by modern and contemporary thinkers and writers. Blanchot, I believe, illuminates most completely and ingeniously what is entailed in the writing of ineffability – the writing that arises from the experience of an impossibility of expression in language. He thus helps us understand the purport of Dante's project in the *Paradiso*.

Without this understanding, we may well find ourselves wishing, as does Robert Hollander, among Dante's most accomplished critics, that Dante had repeated himself a little less frequently, that his relentless reiterations of the ineffability topos had been curtailed, or at least more contained. We will not fully comprehend why precisely this is essentially what the poem is about and not rather an untoward circumstance that slows down its progress. The contents of the poem are fascinating in themselves, but they fascinate in the way the Medusa does: Dante does all he can to force us beyond them to the essential experience that cannot be processed by the usual critical methods for inventorying the poem's plethora of representations.

Historically accurate insight is not all that we stand to gain by studying Dante. There is a further task of mediating Dante's gnoseological venture through our own current search for understanding. We have to appropriate and adapt Dante's terms in order to understand them in their full philosophical significance. To do so, it is appropriate and even necessary to examine our vocabularies for linguistic creation and interpretation in light of the most fully developed concepts of philosophy available to us today. These concepts are always already operative in any case, with or without our awareness, but an explicit theoretical examination can sharpen our understanding of crucial aspects of the problematic of language and its limits – and thereby of Dante's undertaking in its relevance to our own contemporary quest for religious and poetic insight.

My reading of the *Paradiso* through Blanchot and other French thinkers of difference is also intended to reflect critically on the latter. Dante's vision cannot be simply appropriated and absorbed by the outlook of more recent thinkers. Reading contemporary thought through Dante can also show what is tragically lacking in thinking that is otherwise brilliant and clairvoyant. Bataille, Blanchot, Derrida and company (especially their epigones) have occasionally seemed to interpret the Open or the Outside nihilistically, as if 'nothing' were the last word rather than an opening to a fathomless beyond, an Outside that we can never be finished with wording anew, as impossible as it proves to be. Some of them sometimes seem to have lost the sense of certain aspects of the theological mystery harbouring here – especially of the positive theology that necessarily accompanies the negative. Atheism is typically the bias they express when pushed, although they are usually well aware of the pitfalls and vanity of defining their position in such terms.[3] Such a position is perfectly possible, but it is a decision and is not simply imposed by the nature of things. It is a decision of faith. All are entitled to their own biases and beliefs in matters that entail not just objective judgements but also decisions and commitments determining our overall orientation and belonging.

4

The Step/Not Beyond

The *pas au-delà* or 'step beyond', as Blanchot employs it, is also a 'step *not* beyond', since *pas* in French means 'not' as well as 'step'. 'Pas' is a particle of negation as well as a substantive noun signifying 'step'. Transcendence, this suggests, is intrinsically a negation of its own going beyond (*au-delà*): a 'step/not'. Yet, negation that negates even itself is not quite negation. For Blanchot, it is not quite anything. It 'is' what Blanchot calls the neuter (*le neutre*). It can be ferreted out by a neither/nor sort of negation that leaves nothing defined but only an undefined Nothing or no-thing in the excluded middle that escapes both negation and affirmation. It opens to an Outside.

The 'step/not beyond' is an ambiguous step beyond, an ambiguous transcendence which is also *not* transcendence, *not* beyond or *au-delà*. This is worked out one way for Blanchot, as also for Dante, in terms of the idea that eternity is the not beyond of time: eternity is to be experienced *in* time, in time's breaking open or fissuring, in an ungraspable moment in its midst. In the vocabulary of the *pas au-delà*, Blanchot writes of a 'step beyond', leading out of time, yet falling still within it:

> Time, time: the step beyond which is not accomplished in time would lead out of time, not, however, in such a way that this outside should be atemporal; rather it leads to where time would fall, a fragile fall, according to this 'out of time within time' towards which writing would attract us, if it were permitted us, having disappeared as us, to write under the sway of the secret of the ancient fear.
>
> *Temps, temps: le pas au-delà qui ne s'accomplit pas dans le temps conduirait hors du temps, sans que ce dehors fût intemporel, mais là où le temps tomberait, chute fragile, selon ce 'hors temps dans le temps' vers lequel écrire nous attirerait, s'il nous était permis, disparus de nous, d'écrire sous le secret de la peur ancienne.*[1]

This is a step not realized temporally, and yet all steps that are taken in time are dependent on it. It is more primordial than the 'we', which disappears into it. In this impossible step, the 'we' disappears, as we are attracted by the Outside, even as we fall under the spell of 'the ancient fear'.

Analogously, in the *Paradiso*, the transcendence of language, at least in a first approach and acceptation, is to be conceived of not as wholly without or apart from language but rather as immanent to it. It is the transcendence *of* language – in this case a subjective as well as an objective genitive – where language remains the means and medium that actively accomplishes its own transcendence. In this sense, language is not left behind. It remains the protagonist of a transcendence that is specifically linguistic and poetic and that recasts the metaphysical system of theology in experiential terms – in terms of the experience of language.

This temporal experience, or experience of time in its non-origin and in its dispersion through writing, as in the scattering of Sibyl's leaves evoked by Dante, is at the same time an intimation of eternity. This happens especially in the moments of *failure* to express that inhabit and haunt Dante's *Paradiso* from the beginning to the end. Dante experiences eternity in the aporias of language that interrupt narrative time, forcing his pen to 'jump' (*Par.* XXIV.25) or constraining his poetic prowess to 'desist' (*Par.* XXX.31) and acknowledge its helplessness.

Dante is expressing the aporetic aspect of a tradition of speculation that discovered eternity *in* time – or as the outside of time within it. Early on, Saint Augustine, drawing on Plotinus, found eternity to be the abiding presence of the Present in the passing of time from past to future, and the paradigm for this discovery was language. The recital of a verse of a psalm, in Augustine's example, realizes the unified meaning of the sentence in and through the succession of syllables pronounced in time. The meaning of the verse exists independently before and after the recitation of the psalm – and yet is realized only in and through time and its succession of disappearing moments.[2]

The aporia of time is treated by Augustine through an analogy to language. And the paradox that continuity can be established only by discontinuity (just as Creation must be founded on a transcendent God) is presented by Dante likewise in terms of language. Dante takes a step beyond language and yet remains within it and faces its origin in the secret of the ancient fear – or perhaps equivalently in the anxiety vis-à-vis nothing. The approach to the divinity is fear-arousing, especially when the divinity can be defined by no known characteristics. As such, it has been treated traditionally as the *mysterium tremendum*.[3]

The force of Dante's language is in its 'neutrality', its being neither outside time nor within it, and its being neither transcendent nor immanent, but rather transcendent in its immanence.[4] Dante, too, experiences this transcendence of language within language – as the neuter, language as neutered, as manifesting what it cannot qualify or contain. Language opens upon what is altogether without qualities. As such, Dante's 'vision' is simply the linguistic without qualification – which for him could not but be a theological description. It is the Word beyond words. This neuter of language is without definable qualities, and that is what produces the 'ancient fear', a fear of the indefinable.

Blanchot's 'neuter', as unqualified being or No-thing, fulfils a role coinciding with that of God for Dante and for medieval theology, at least within the apophatic or negative theological culture transmitted by the Middle Ages. Everything is potentially there (and not there) in the unqualified neuter – something like the way the Neoplatonic One is all inclusive: it is all things as their emanating source and yet itself is nothing, no one (or none) of the things that are. Analogously, in the conception of medieval mathematics, the One is understood as the neutral number par excellence: further numbers are subtractions from the One rather than additions to it.[5] The One is transcendentally present or immanent in everything that is, though nowhere present or utterable as itself.

The immanence to language of Dante's experience of Paradise has been fairly well recognized. It can be approached from many different angles and has been proposed not infrequently in criticism of the last canticle.[6] Treating it, furthermore, explicitly as a modality of transgression, James Miller emphasizes the paradox that Dante's penchant for ineffability is an enabling condition of his rhetorical abundance. The fullness of speech is the expression of an impasse to proper language and to adequate expression: 'His fallback to speechless wonder is playfully ironic: what the ineffability topos is meant to signal here is, as usual, the very opposite of what it literally means. How carefully and covertly he has trained us through nearly a hundred cantos of unsurpassable rhetorical virtuosity to read the temporary "failure" of his words as a cue for the imminent triumph of speech over silence – the ecstatic silence that paradoxically gives rise to the inexhaustible "effability" of the Sacred Poem!'[7]

There is something right about this: ineffability is in its own way loquacious.[8] And yet surely there is more to Dante's ineffability than just a coy ploy to cover over false modesty while actually his eloquence triumphs. The idea that Paradise *is* essentially the experience of poetic language is an argument for immanence, on the one hand. Dante's Paradise is immanent to his poem, the *Paradiso*. On the other hand, poetic language is itself a step beyond – beyond even itself. It is broken open to an Outside; it is the opening to a beyond. That is the essential nature (beyond essence and nature) of language as Dante's *Paradiso* discovers– or rather invents– it. For Dante, this does not prevent theological reappropriations of the beyond and the Outside. The metaphors of Trinity and Incarnation in particular are used by him all the way to the end as revelations of the transcendent Word. Of course, they remain *metaphors* in Dante's poetic discourse – metaphors more true than any plainly fact-stating discourse could be – for what remains stubbornly intractable to every sort of linguistic treatment.[9]

Blanchot, in contrast, is determined to evade any such theological reappropriations. Nevertheless, this avoidance must not resort to exclusion by simple negation. Blanchot's disavowal of theology is a never-ending disappropriation that continually reinstates an appropriation that it forever refuses. Blanchot's refusal of theology is, in actuality, an 'infinite conversation' with theology. Dante's metaphors, conversely, are disappropriations as much as appropriations of theology, for they do not affirm a proper theological sense as independently ascertainable and normative. Theological vision takes place rather in the experience of poetic language. Dante does not finally subordinate poetry to theology as another discourse of a more scientific, truer kind.[10]

The idea of the step/not beyond is that the negation is really the beyond. If one dwells in it rather than passing immediately beyond to another positive term that is presumably not negated, one dwells in what we have called the neuter, and this is beyond affirmations and negations and beyond positive terms altogether. It is where they all come from – and also where they inevitably go. It cuts to the world of things in their emergence before they have become what they definitely, definably are. Negation, inasmuch as it negates even itself and thus refuses to issue in any new, merely positive affirmation, leaves things in a fluid state freed from all supervening determinations.

This is something that Dante in his way, too, is manifesting in his impossible representations of Paradise. His language abides always in the creative moment of emergence in which 'everything becomes what it is' (*ciascuna cosa qual ell'è diventa, Par.* XX.78), a moment which proves impossible to express definitively. Such language admits its own defeat, yet has, nevertheless, performed its indispensable service in its very failure to represent its supposed object. Any crystallized form of expression is surpassed and superseded even before it has been fully achieved. It is the neutered expression of no-thing that has become manifest – as we shall see.

By introducing such a vocabulary, I do not mean to suggest that we cannot understand Dante without Blanchot, but Blanchot is among those who push our contemporary understanding of the unsayable in language to its furthest limits. Therefore, the juxtaposition of these two brilliantly original explorers of the unsayable is particularly revealing. It creates a synergism between Dante's late poetic work and the thought of difference in recent French philosophy. Each can elucidate the other.

Attempts to read Dante through French critical theory to date have concentrated predominantly on Derrida. The relevance of *difference* to Dante is patent and has been pursued by divergent critical projects.[11] Interesting insight into Dante has been gained by these Derridean readings. However, it is Blanchot, who thinks essentially through literature and who, therefore, is most apt to lend us the analogues for interpreting, in a language of contemporary critical theory, Dante's final experience in Paradise of impasse itself as the passage beyond. Dante's deeper affinities are with Blanchot and his approach to the Absolute through the experience of literature.

I have previously argued that hermeneutic theory best illuminates, from a contemporary philosophical perspective, the project of the *Commedia*. However, this is so *before* the poem takes the turn it does in the *Paradiso*, in which this project places itself in question and performs a sort of self-subversion, in order to attain a goal beyond its own reach.[12] The articulation in postmodern times between modern hermeneutic thought, which strives to forge a horizon for unlimited, universal understanding, and the thought of difference, which insists on impasses to such universal understanding, is homologous to something in the shape of Dante's intellectual journey. Dante works in the transition from the high Scholasticism of the age of Aquinas to the radical apophaticism of Meister Eckhart. An epochal shift can be discerned in his work and in that of his generation, which includes also other apophatic geniuses such as Abraham Abulafia.[13] Both trajectories – Dante's own and the intellectual history of his time – delineate a progression from the construction of a comprehensive vision to its collapse – and the consequent peering through its cracks to what lies beyond vision. In the case of the *Paradiso*, the vision is actually in and of language – and the collapse of this linguistic system opens to a beyond of language and of vision.[14]

In Dante, the beyond of language is linguistically determined in a way that is not always the case in apophatic mysticism. Dante forges, in effect, a *language mysticism*. His transcending of language through mystical ascent results in a more intense immanence to language – namely, the full linguistic intensity of the *Paradiso*. Precisely, this movement instantiates the paradoxical logic of the *pas au-delà*. Language is absolutized even in being transcended: the transcendent becomes manifest essentially in the immanence of language. Language remains essential to Dante's *Paradiso* even and *especially* in being transcended. The aim of most mystics, presumably, is to inhabit silence without words. It is just that we do not hear much about them – or at least not *from* them. We *do* hear from Dante, whose paradoxical transcendence-immanence (which turns out to be neither exactly one nor the other) can be pursued best – and perhaps only – in terms of the neuter.

5

The Neuter – Nothing Except Nuance

We can begin to approach the non-concept of the neuter, as used by Blanchot, etymologically through the Latin expression *ne uter*, 'neither one'.[1] The neuter is the movement away from all determinations to their indeterminate and indeterminable ground. It is the non-sense that makes sense possible – or more precisely, what is between all the senses that can be defined and stated. Accordingly, it is manifest as 'neither x, nor y, nor z' and so on. It is not simply negation, which produces a negative form of whatever is negated, but negation of each and every determinate form repeated recursively *ad infinitum*. This formula delineates a function of never completed negating or 'othering' that determines not a concept that can be defined (and so made definitive) or be thought as such, but a procedure of transformation, to which concepts can and must be submitted without end. This is a procedure less of knowing than of non-knowing or *non-savoir* – a crucial common concern of Blanchot and Bataille.

Christophe Bident suggests that the neuter, given its originally grammatical connotation and matrix, may be 'the written form of non-knowledge' (p. 17) that is reminiscent of Nothing (*le RIEN*). He points to Blanchot's focus on the 'ineffable power' of an unnameable 'obscure presence' in his first published piece of literary criticism.[2] The neuter is the absence of sense (*l'absence de sense*), and yet as such it has a sort of transcendental role as a condition of the possibility of sense. 'No ontological, ethical, or linguistic discourse would be feasible without the *absence of sense* that the neuter manifests, and of which it is the sole manifestation' (Bident, p. 23). The neuter's role is further defined by Bident as being to stave off or 'keep at bay' the nihilism of the negative, to evade the negative sense created by negation. This parallels and reproduces, I submit, the vocation of negative theology to save theology from becoming *simply* or terminally negative. In effect, negative theology saves the Name of God – as in Derrida's *Sauf le nom* – as ineffable precisely by undermining all inevitably idolatrous formulations of it. While rendering all possible, yet remaining itself neutral and in no way determined, the neuter transcends every positive or negative determination.

Such an apophatic a-logic of the neuter is broached in perhaps its most accessible form by Roland Barthes. The topic was already central for Barthes in his widely read *Writing Degree Zero* (*Le dégrée zéro de l'écriture*, 1953), as the title itself attests. Barthes's reflections on the neuter as escaping from binary oppositions between contrary terms and thus as designed to foil paradigms (*déjouer les paradigms*) were formative for Blanchot, and they can be illuminating for anyone trying to get a handle on this necessarily most elusive of notions. Barthes further developed his notion of the neuter later in life and in contact particularly with Oriental apophaticism. His late thinking, subsequent to his trip to China in 1974, reconceives this notion under the pervasive influence of Zen Buddhism and Taoism.

In 1978, Barthes gave a series of lectures at the Collège de France dedicated to *le neutre*.[3] The main title of the translation of this lecture course, 'The Neutral', can be misleading, since Barthes makes very clear that the neuter as he understands it is anything but neutral in the usual sense: it is the opposite of indifference or tepidness. It is ardent and intense, yet not partisan for one side or the other of any divisive binaries. It is characterized by the greatest commitment, yet commitment which cannot be discerned within the hierarchical, oppositional terms imposed by society and its power structures.

Barthes rather winsomely considers the neuter as *nuance*, for a nuance cannot quite be identified with any positive quality. A nuance of flavour or colour can be specified without defining exactly *what* it is a nuance *of*. It is a specific difference that can make all the difference, yet it is only an inflection of something else that as such remains unknown and perhaps even indeterminate in itself. Only the nuance indicates that there is something – one really does not know what – of which it is the nuance.

I believe that this is what Paul Verlaine intuits in *Ars poétique*, which intriguingly speaks of the art of poetry as requiring 'nothing but nuance' (*rien que la nuance*):

> *Car nous voulons la Nuance encor,*
> *Pas la Couleur, rien que la nuance!*
> *Oh ! la nuance seule fiance*
> *Le rêve au rêve et la flûte au cor!*

> Because we want the Nuance again,
> Not the color, nothing but the nuance!
> O the nuance alone betroths
> Dream to dream and flute to horn!

More directly perhaps than Verlaine's poetics, Barthes's poetic way of taking the neuter can readily be aligned with negative theology. In fact, Barthes invokes the negative theologies of Dionysius the Areopagite and Gregory of Nyssa as referring to *agape* penetrated by *eros* to form a neutral love between the two, a love consisting in ecstatic desire that can be qualified as arising neither out of charity (as in *agape*) nor out of need (as in *eros*). Love at its intensest is neutred by these two conflicting conceptualities which, taken together, fail to account for it. What is love? Perhaps nothing that can be said – and in any case, more than anything that can be given just a determinate sense.

Among Barthes's principal theses is the idea that 'sense rests upon conflict' (*Le sens repose sur le conflit*). Making sense demands difference and divisiveness: dividing A from not-A is the minimum condition for any definable sense. And this is what the neuter resists doing. We might say, for example, that there is a nuance of spring in the air. And we can do so without committing ourselves to saying that it actually *is* spring or any other season, and even without saying that what is called 'air' actually is or is not air in any true sense of the word (or false one, for that matter). Saying that there is a nuance of spring in the air is an affirmation that erases all its presumable presuppositions. There is something that serves us to discern a nuance of spring, but whether the 'something' in question is or is not air or spring or anything else remains moot. What the nuance is a nuance *of* need not be determined in order for the nuance of 'spring' to be felt in the circumambient 'air' – or whatever it is in which we live and move and have our being. To think in terms of the neuter is to remain cognizant that all determinations of sense, just like the assertions of power they are used to ground, are at the deepest ontological level suspended upon a void. Any ultimate ground like God has to be beyond all determinate sense that we can make of it. Our sense-making can produce only idols.

Among the most powerful motivations of Dante's overall vision of the world and history, one source-spring of his thought can be found in his burning desire to transcend partisan conflict. He is moved from the anguished depths of his personal experience shaken by internecine conflict resulting in his exile to embrace an ideal of peaceful coexistence in harmonious community among humans. Dante's entire *oeuvre* is saturated with this ideal, which he presents theoretically and systematically in his treatise on government, *De monarchia*. A call to peace also happens to be the heart of the Christian vision, even as interpreted by that most cantankerous of contemporary Christian theologians, John Milbank.[4] Adopting in particular the terms of mystical and apophatic theology that had blossomed in his own time, with Meister Eckhart and Abraham Abulafia, at what could be considered its high point in the Middle Ages, Dante realized that in order to inaugurate a genuine and universal peace, he had to dismantle or escape from paradigms of binary opposition. He was engaged in conflict throughout his life, but he evolved in his thought towards envisioning a language that would exit from this grid of oppositions and, in a sense, exit from language altogether. This is the goal towards which Dante finally directs his poetic project and his life's endeavours: it can be understood in our own contemporary critical terms as a desire for the neuter.

In order to connect the neuter with God, one thing is necessary and sufficient: to give up all pretensions to have any notion that adequately comprehends God – precisely as in the tradition of negative theology from Gregory of Nyssa and Dionysius through Aquinas and Eckhart. The neuter is the precondition of all sense: it is prior to every sense – to sense and non-sense alike. It 'haunts' sense with a ghostly presence that is never presented in itself or as such but always only in alien guises. It is like the root of sense in a family of words that is not itself any word or sense but rather 'the unidentifiable surplus' (*le surplus inidentifiable*, L'entretien infini, p. 450) that lends sense to them all. Like the God of the ontological argument, the neuter is always in excess of being. Blanchot himself makes this connection (p. 448). Whether God is or is not, God remains God and these affirmations or denials are made within determinations of the sense of 'God', who Himself withdraws from any definite sense assigned, whether as existing or as inexistent. The neuter is like literature in suspending whatever it presents, making it as fiction and placing it between inverted commas, yet giving it a status of its own that escapes from the alternative real/not real and from all such alternatives assigning a determinate sense.

The neuter, in effect, entails an erasure of the positive determinations of being, as one penetrates beyond them into the experience of what cannot be said. We find it at work most crucially in another baffling but compelling image – that of Forgetting. This is the image that Dante offers at the end of his poem for how its whole linguistic-symbolic system collapses – and is thereby also transfigured and indeed transcended.

6

Forgetting and the Limits of Experience – *Letargo* and the *Argo*

In addition to the leaves of Sibyl, another emblem of how the totalizing symbolic system of the poem comes undone in the end is the reference to Forgetting in the final canto. A colossal work of synthetic imagination, of the Muses and of Memory, the poem recognizes itself *in finis* as arriving at a Forgetting – at what entails the undoing or letting go of the whole elaborate mnemonic construction of the *Comedy*. As he approaches his final vision of God, whom he has just described as a simple point of light (*un semplice lume*, XXXIII.90), Dante surprisingly – and, for many, shockingly – evokes a single point of immense 'forgetting' (*letargo*, from the Greek *lethe*, forgetfulness):

> *Un punto solo m'è maggior letargo*
> *che venticinque secoli a la 'mpresa*
> *che fé Nettuno ammirar l'ombra d'Argo.*
> (*Par.* XXXIII.94–6)
> A single point to me is greater forgetting
> than twenty-five centuries since the venture
> that made Neptune marvel at the shadow of the Argo.

This point – God, in Dante's vision – entails a greater forgetting than that of the two and a half millennia since recorded history opened with the first sea voyage, that of Jason and the Argonauts. In medieval traditions, Jason's voyage often counted as inaugurating human history by undertaking a technical feat in excess of nature and braving its boundaries. All of history is supposed to be a revelation of God in Dante's Christian providential perspective, and yet here Dante looks beyond or behind or before history towards what is more primordial than anything history can remember, towards what is prior to the revelation or disclosedness in which history consists. He suggests that all forms of anamnesis through historical representation come from a deeper source in Forgetting and that all cultural representations must finally be forgotten in order to gain access to our deepest source and origin. In fact, culture and its representations quite generally are exposed as intrinsically forms of forgetting of this deeper source. Dante is groping after the God who is not capable of being remembered or represented and yet makes possible remembering, along with all that is remembered – or in any way *is*.

The poem does not finally triumph in the recovery for memory of Dante's comprehensive cultural history. Rather, he experiences the supreme moment of vision as equivalent to the *loss* of two and a half millennia of history – starting from the journey of the Argonauts that began the history of audacious human exploits of which Dante's journey is the latest instalment and culminating episode. In this respect, it is forgetting that confers its final sense on the poem. Dante's ultimate vision is represented as a non-vision, as blessed obliviousness!

Dante's qualifying the end (and therewith also the origin) of his poem as a Forgetting can be difficult to accept – as Robert Hollander's survey of the commentary tradition on these verses demonstrates. It has proven to be and has remained, according to Hollander, one of the most difficult points in the whole poem to interpret in any satisfying way.[1] Nevertheless, it is hardly unparalleled in the Middle Ages, especially in this period's pervasive apophatic or mystical and negative-theological countercurrents. Dante's forgetting can be plausibly linked to the cessation of all intellectual and sensual activities in the 'excessus mentis' in which Bonaventure's *Itinerarium mentis in Deum* culminates.[2] In the supreme moment, in the apex of its desire or affections, the soul ceases to function as an individual consciousness and is, in effect, transformed into God (*opportet quod relinquantur omnes intellectuales operationes, et apex affectus totus transferetur et transformetur in Deum*, VII.4). This mystic experience remains recalcitrant to being grasped and digested rationally and must simply be acknowledged.

That the moment of total vision, which is the goal towards which Dante's poem moves, should be reached, incredibly, through forgetting touches on a philosophical paradox that calls for elucidation also through certain radical reflections of contemporary thought concerning the enigma of forgetting as the necessary condition of remembering. Blanchot writes of 'the relation with a profound immemorial memory, one which originates in the "fabulous" times before history, in the epoch in which man seems to recall what he has never known. . . . if he remembers, it is by forgetting' (*ce rapport avec la profonde mémoire immémoriale, celle qui prend origine dans les temps 'fabuleux', en deçà de l'histoire, à cette époque où l'homme semble se rappeler ce qu'il n'a jamais su. . . . s'il se souvient, c'est par oubli,* L'entretien infini, p. 464).

This comment unwittingly glosses the role of the tale of the Argonauts in Dante's verses on the threshold of a fabulous prehistory that resurfaces only with the forgetting of all the intervening time of history. In his final vision, Dante encounters a greater forgetting (*maggior letargo*) than the twenty-five centuries (*venticinque secoli*) of remembered history – all of which counts first as a forgetting. The vision of God, the single 'point', is a forgetting like and, in fact, disproportionately greater than the whole of recorded history – all that has happened since the mythic or legendary time of the Argonauts' voyage, which marks the limit of historical memory.

Blanchot likewise gives priority to Forgetting over Memory – it is profounder. It is the older divinity from which Mnemosyne is engendered a generation later.[3] It is of mythic proportions – or rather disproportion. Profoundly considered, all the representations of memory are but rays reflected back from the black sun of Forgetting. Only Forgetting retains the deep source and the whole of what any remembering inevitably forgets. Only Forgetting can gather language together as a whole and hold it around the word that has slipped from memory: 'Forgetting raises language as a whole in gathering it around the forgotten word' (*L'oubli soulève le langage dans son ensemble en le rassemblant autour du mot oublié*, p. 289). Language thereby evokes a space or emptiness that is its origin and wholeness. Blanchot observes that searching for a word we cannot remember can be an experience not just of trying to plug a hole, but more profoundly of feeling out an abyss:

> When we lack a forgotten word, it designates itself still by this lack; we have it *as* forgotten and thus we reaffirm it in this absence which it seems to be made for, in order to fill and dissimulate its place. In the forgotten word, we grasp the space from which it speaks and which now directs us to its mute sense, unavailable, interdicted, and always latent.
>
> *Quand un mot oublié nous manque, il se désigne encore par ce manque; nous l'avons comme oublié et ainsi le réaffirmons dans cette absence qu'il ne semblait fait que pour remplir et en dissimuler la place. Dans le mot oublié, nous saisissons l'espace à partir duquel il parle et qui maintenant nous renvoie à son sens muet, indisponible, interdit et toujours latent.*[4]

Blanchot further explains that 'to forget a word is to encounter the possibility that every word might be forgotten and to hold oneself near to every word as forgotten and also near to memory as a word' (*Oublier un mot, c'est rencontrer la possibilité que toute parole soit oubliée, se tenir auprès de toute parole comme oubliée et aussi auprès de l'oubli comme parole*, p. 289).

Memory is a word: Dante's journey travels through the words of his poem, and the very distinction between the journey and the poem seems progressively to attenuate. The word issues finally in silence, and memory is extinguished in forgetting. Such are the negations that come at the climax of the quest, whether it is considered as mystical or as literary: rather than completion through progressive accumulation, finally a reversal of sense and even a turning of sense into non-sense are necessary to cross the threshold from the finite to the infinite. The fulfillment of the quest cannot come just through more of the same in a mere accumulation, but only through a qualitative leap to an altogether other kind of measure – or rather measurelessness.

Forgetting gathers all language around what is unknown and indistinct – or more precisely, forgotten. Essential forgetting is itself an abyss without origin, yet it gathers all remembering and re-presenting around itself. In this relation, all memory is like a work forgotten. Blanchot conceives of forgetting as prior, as preceding there being anything distinct to recollect. Such essential forgetting is referred to a past that never was present. System, law, definition *tout court* are transgressed and even obliterated by this recuperation of the 'terribly ancient'. Law only begins with the separation of good and evil and the ordering of chaos into distinct elements. But essential forgetting gives access to – or at least turns upon – what is prior to all that. It is essentially different from the piece-meal assemblage of remembering – the art that the god Asclepius, who teaches humans medicine, practices in putting back together the *disiecta membra* of Hippolytus. We are reminded that the Greek word for truth, *aletheia*, is built upon *lethe*, forgetting. Truth or disclosure or revelation is merely a modification in an underlying, all-embracing economy of oblivion.

The vision of God, rather than conferring lucidly objective consciousness, plunges Dante into the deepest forgetting, just as all that is remembered and valued by us as history is also equated to a forgetting. There is something else that is covered over by all our cultural memory, and that mysterious 'something' is more valuable and vital than anything memory can contain. For Dante, of course, everything comes from God, and yet he is able to directly experience God himself only in the luminous darkness of unknowing and forgetting, the *lux tenebrosa* of Dionysius the Areopagite's *Mystical Theology*: this 'night' lies just behind any positive representations that he can imagine or experience. Blanchot's 'night', in contrast, knows no God and cannot know one, for a God would reinvest everything with sense. And then it would not be outside all cultural constructions. And yet the unknowability of God is the point also of the Christian apophatic tradition from which Dante's sense of the mystic ascent to 'vision' hails. Dante and Christians have their reasons for believing that all things come from God rather than simply from night, yet Christians too must acknowledge the necessity of passage through night – as in John of the Cross's dark night of the soul ("la noche oscura") – in the journey towards direct experience of the ultimate source that no one can naturally know or know in essence.

Beyond the origin of the order of the cosmos, Dante too intuits the nothing (no thing that is defined or finite) from which all this comes, and he recognizes that *it* is as much an image of God as are all our theological descriptions – or even more so. In his gesture at the end of his poem, Dante transgresses all laws of form and order in his fidelity to their source. This source is a transcendence which can never be adequately represented by any human means, certainly not by any concept such as 'transcendence'. It is encountered rather in the breakdown and scattering of all images and revelations – strewn like the leaves of Sibyl – and in the forgetting of all of history, everything since the *Argo*. This Forgetting first opens the way to the Mind of God. For God grasps all as it 'is' before history begins. In the end, the whole of cultural history that Dante's poem so brilliantly summarizes and synthesizes is precisely what *separates* us from All as gathered into its (to us) dark source or womb. More deeply considered, all these historical and represented memories are forms of forgetting of the unattainable Origin that can be indicated only by acknowledging this Forgetting.

Blanchot points out that a forgotten word renders the 'latency' from which it speaks (*Entretien infini*, p. 289). The word we are missing signifies by virtue of a lack which is open in the direction of a latent background or matrix. More than any finite ideas or concepts, the Infinite and the whole of language and its ultimate source are evoked by this forgetting. Dante's intuition of this dynamic is registered in provocative metaphorical figures. The reference to the scattering of Sibyl's leaves is one of the clearest piercings through to what lies behind the veil of representation – which in a dramatic denouement turns out to be the goal of the whole poem. This 'beyond' is the Infinite, and despite all Dante's heroic efforts to represent it, in the end it eludes him. It is rendered only through his release of all the representations and images that the poem furnishes in such abundance. It is their scattering and forgetting that ultimately achieves Dante's meaning – or rather his going beyond meaning, with its definitions and delimitations, towards its abyssal ground: he can arrive at his goal only by erasing meaning and its inevitably finite representations, since they are inadequate to the infinite and divine.

The scattering and forgetting in question are transgressions and destructions of the entire regime of poetic representation and theological revelation of truth that subtend Dante's poem and its intellectual and cultural tradition. It is through resolutely transgressing every order of presentation and representation that Dante finally delivers his divine vision. Most deeply understood, it is a non-vision – which, nevertheless, in its very forgetfulness casts a shadow of infinitely rich and nuanced images that are glimpsed in the act of disappearing.

Like Jason on his unprecedented journey, Dante at the outset of the *Paradiso* ventures out upon the great sea of being (*il gran mar dell'essere*, I.13). Dante's voyage is apprehended and can be conveyed only through the shadow it casts in his mind (*l'ombra del beato regno/segnato nel mio capo*, I.23-4). Similarly, all that is seen of Jason's passing is his ship's shadow – *l'ombra d'Argo*. This is a figure for Dante's voyage, too, which is perceived not directly in itself, but only by means of the shadow it casts in language, for the rest is hidden, even from Dante himself, in the invisible. The same holds for the whole paradisiacal realm that this voyage traverses: it is seen only in negative – as its own shadow cast in language. This, at any rate, is all that can appear to the 'sight' of language, since language works by difference, without ever presenting positive terms that are intelligible purely in themselves. This apparently holds even for the god Neptune, who in gazing upon a human journey into the unknown sees but a *shadow*.

The divine vision is realized as God's own vision – subjectively rather than objectively. Dante's simile reverses the point of view: God himself, in the figure of Neptune, stares in admiration. Subject and object have traded places. Dante is no longer looking at God; rather, a god is looking at him, the voyager. This is a point about the vision of God that Nicholas of Cusa, among philosophers in the speculative tradition of negative theology, was particularly fond of stressing: the *visio Dei* is ultimately God's own vision.[5] Vision of God as object is not possible, but vision of objects in their truth and as totally revealed is the way God sees them. So this is, in effect, 'the vision of God'. Of course, finite human vision cannot sustain such infinitely objective vision – except perhaps momentarily through grace. Furthermore, that this 'seeing' takes place for Dante concretely in language, in the language of poetry, gives it all a metaphorical status. This is hinted at in the fact that the divine vision (Neptune's sight) is only of a shadow: 'l'*ombra* d'Argo'. In fact, all vision of God can be only of shadows, indeed not literally vision at all.

In some sense, Dante's images all along are forgettings, inasmuch as they are shadows and prefaces (*umbriferi prefazii*, XXX.78) of something else that is not present. Will it then ever become present? Not in time, but Dante and his tradition teach us to live time as oriented towards and open upon something that time does not comprehend. His language – and that of biblical and religious traditions generally – for this beyond of time speaks of the eternal. How do we remember eternity? By unremembering time – or by letting go of all its accumulations at just the point where we would finally achieve the completeness we have been striving after on our struggle to recollect our vanished origin. And yet Dante remains nevertheless a Titan second to none in his dedication to the work of memory that leads up to this moment.

Indeed Dante's *Commedia* has frequently been taken as a paradigmatic realization of the *ars memoriae* elaborated in ancient rhetoric, according to which the contents of memory were cast into forms of images that were then ranged mentally in a space familiar to, or at any rate visualizable by, the individual constructing the memory. Some decades ago, Frances Yates wrote: 'That Dante's *Inferno* could be regarded as a kind of memory system . . . will come as a great shock, and I must leave it as a shock'.[6] However, taking Dante as the culmination of the ancient rhetorical tradition of the *ars memorativa* is actually an idea that has a considerable history in critical theory and comparative literature. Ernst Robert Curtius's book on European literature in the Latin Middle Ages suggested that the *Divine Comedy* embodies exemplarily the art of memory as cultivated in the teachings of ancient rhetoricians such as Cicero and Quintilian.⁷ Indeed, this art subtends even more broadly Dante's entire *oeuvre* from the *incipit* of his youthful *Vita nuova*, which begins with the trope of the 'book of memory' (*il libro de la mia memoria*, I.i).

The mnemonological aspects of Dante's work have even become the subject of a discrete sub-field of Dante studies that is outlined by Harald Weinrich in his 1994 address to the Accademia della Crusca on *La memoria di Dante*.⁸ The theme had been broached by Weinrich already in 1990 in his inaugural lecture at the Collège de France. In *La mémoire linguistique de l'Europe*, Weinrich characterizes the *Divine Comedy* as a 'vast mnemonic system' (*un vaste système mnémonique*), 'the most magisterial of courses in poetic memnotechnics' (*le cours de mnémotechnie poétique le plus magistral*), representing the culmination of the Art of Memory developed in the ancient rhetorical tradition of the Rhetoric of Herennium, Cicero and Quintilian.⁹

In *Lethe: Kunst und Kritik des Vergessens*, Weinrich turns his attention to Forgetting as the mighty threat that Dante's monumental literary 'cathedral' is built to stave off – it stands against oblivion's having its way with the frailty of human memory (*dann kann das Vergessen nicht mehr sein übliches Spiel mit dem Menschengedächtnis treiben*).¹⁰ Thus, Dante's *oeuvre* and particularly the *Divina Commedia* are treated as an art of memory designed to overcome forgetting (*Wir haben nämlich in Dantes* Divina Commedia *ein genaues literarisches Abbild der antiken Gedächtniskunst [ars memoriae] vor uns*, p. 43). The *Commedia* is composed of memory contents deposited as images in an organized array of places (*topoi*). The meticulously articulated divisions and subdivisions of the landscapes of *Inferno* and *Purgatorio*, as well as the hierarchically ordered planetary spheres and stellar spaces of the *Paradiso*, offer grids of exactly the kind necessary for the practice of the traditional art of memory as laid out in the theoretical treatises of the rhetorical tradition passing through Cicero and Quintilian to Saint Augustine.

It is in some sense God's mind or memory (*memoria Dei*, als *genitives subjectivus*) that Dante travels through in the world beyond the grave

(Weinrich, *Lethe*, p. 44). The art of memory based on the classical tradition from Homer and Plato and Ovid is combined with biblical tradition when it passes through Augustine's theory – expounded in Book X of the *Confessions* – of finding God again in a part of memory that forgetting and sin and consequent corruption could not erase. However, if the *Commedia* is designed to be a gigantic construction of memory, one that, as representing the memory of God, is totalizing and in principle infallibly true, what Dante signals at the end of his journey is its failure. He cannot in the end achieve his goal through memory, however powerful, but only through forgetting. It is through giving up the effort to complete the construction of the cathedral of memory, through forsaking it in surrender to forgetting, that he can finally somehow touch upon – or be touched by – the divine consciousness with which he enters into mystical union.[11]

One needs a negative art of memory, or rather an art of forgetfulness, in order to appreciate this necessary reversal of the cultural bias to privilege always memory over its opposite. Such an *ars oblivionalis*, to use Umberto Eco's term, can be found lurking in the shadows of the tradition of the art of memory or mnemotechnics, although Eco denies its possibility in 'An Ars oblivionalis? Forget It'.[12] Eco's contention is that an art of forgetting is impossible, since any intentional effort to forget cannot but be self-defeating. Leaving intentionality aside, however, the climax of artifice in Dante's poem comes in the ceding of memory in the *Paradiso* before extreme experience, as the poet avows in the final canto: 'and memory gives way faced with such beyondness' (*e cede la memoria a tanto oltraggio*, XXXIII.57). Dante's art in its last and sublimest instance is indeed to forget.

Weinrich, moreover, stresses that one must be freed from memory in order to be blessed: hence the indispensable role of the river Lethe in the afterlife. And yet Weinrich himself remains far short of fully acknowledging Forgetting as the culminating moment and even the goal of the immense *ars memorativa* that is mobilized by the *Commedia*. The poem evinces certain far more radical accents with regard to forgetting than are typically recognized either in the rhetorical tradition or by

Weinrich's cultural history of forgetting. This is what I wish to bring out through contrapuntal exposition with texts by Blanchot.

One finds also in sociologist Marc Augé's *Forms of Forgetting* strong emphasis on how 'forgetting is necessary for society as well as for individuals' (*l'oubli est nécessaire à la société comme à l'individu*) and on how 'forgetting is the principle operator in creating the "fiction" of individual and collective life' (*l'opérateur principal de la mise en 'fiction' de la vie individuelle et collective, c'est l'oubli*).[13] Likewise, philosopher Paul Ricoeur stresses the gaps and forgetting that turn out to be constitutive of memory. Forgetting, separately and in conjunction with pardon, as in amnesty, is the horizon of Ricouer's entire phenomenological study embracing memory and its collective correlate in history (*L'oubli et le pardon désignent, séparément et conjointement, l'horizon de toute notre recherche*).[14]

For Ricoeur, memory traces that survive are themselves all along forms of forgetting. For the inscription of the psychic trace (of what is forgotten) in memory is itself constitutive of lived experience: 'if the live experience was not from the beginning survival of itself, and in this sense a psychic trace, it would never become that.... The inscription, in the psychic sense of the term, is nothing but the survival by itself of the mnemonic image contemporary to the original experience' (*si l'expérience vive n'a pas été dès le début survivance d'elle-même, et en ce sens trace psychique, elle ne le deviendra jamais.... L'inscription, au sens psychique du terme, n'est autre que la survivance par soi de l'image mnémonique contemporaine de l'expérience originaire*, p. 569). The trace in which experience is first registered and retained is not subsequent to but rather coeval with experience itself, and in this sense there is no original experience to be remembered that is not already itself a trace or a retention of forgetting. To this extent, remembering is itself always already a form of forgetting.

Yet there is something still more dark and enigmatic, more subtle and dynamic, about the relation of memory to forgetting that cannot quite be grasped by scientific (sociological) or philosophical (phenomenological) analysis. It can, however, become accessible through literature and in the 'space' surrounding literature (Blanchot's *espace littéraire*). This space can be entered into only by a leap of imagination – and perhaps especially by theological imagination, with its penchant for negating its own concepts in the self-abnegation of thought that believes itself to be surrounded by a knowing greater than its own, one that it cannot quite fathom. This is where Blanchot and Dante can become partners and indispensible guides to an otherwise undiscoverable region at the edge of experience—or just beyond.

As Augustine observed, none of us remembers our beginning: we do not recall being born. Therefore 'that which founds our memory is forever closed and forbidden to memory . . . We began by losing and forgetting' (*ce qui fonde notre mémoire est à jamais clos et interdit à la mémoire . . . . Nous avons commencé par perdre et par oublier*).[15] Jean-Louis Chrétien envisages a forgetting that is not just of a certain 'punctual event' but rather of a dimension that he calls, echoing Blanchot, the 'incessant': it continually impinges on the present, always returning out of a past that never was and so cannot be forgotten (*l'inoubliable*), or anticipating a future that never comes (*l'inespéré*) – as in Blanchot's *L'attente l'oubli* (1962). This dimension of the incessant cuts open and wounds our existence. It exceeds the human, but as immemorial and unhoped for, it exists only by and for humans. Indeed it renders them human. Memory in the ordinary empirical sense is an obstacle rather than an aid to reminiscence of the truth of our essential forgetfulness and incompleteness, our non-coinciding with our origin. To remember this Forgetting constitutes opening to a Truth incommensurable with the human – and this is what Dante achieves at his poem's end.

God is immemorial in being always already with us before we experience him – immemorially, without ever being present or represented. Plotinus, in *Enneads* (V.v.8), suggests that such a truth of Being that has always already come can be known only prophetically through desire of the immemorial. All representation and experience can only be of what is not God Himself, not the ultimate Good or One in person. Dante's final 'vision' is not vision at all but rather remembrance of his ineluctable forgetting of a unity with God that 'precedes' and founds all representation and all experience of anything as present. The Neoplatonic Good of Plotinus similarly escapes all recapture by anamnesis (cf. Chrétien, p. 51). In *Enneads* V.v.12, the Good is present rather in our desire or in our willing the Good: turning ourselves towards it, we are already in it, just as Dante discovers at the very end of his journey that *already* his desire and will (*ma già volgeva il mio disio e 'l velle*, XXXIII.143, cf. line 51) were moving with the Love that moves the universe (*l'amor che move il sole e l'altre stelle*, 145).

7

Speech – The Vision that is Non-Vision

The difference between seeing and saying is vital to the dynamic of the *Paradiso*. The poem offers a prodigious Saying that is all purportedly driven by a *seeing* that it cannot say. Paradoxically, the poem adheres to words tenaciously in the name of what is utterly (and unutterably) beyond words. Dante's pronouncements evoke a Presence that they emphatically *say* cannot be said or represented verbally: it must rather be experienced directly by the individual who wishes to understand (*Par.* I.70–2; X.70-5; XIV.103–108, etc.). Of course, neither can it be 'seen' in any literal sense. We have already examined some indications that only the 'shadow' of what is experienced can be seen, and this shadow consists concretely in language. In this sense at least, the final vision of the poem, of which all the others can be understood to be but partial refractions and preliminary versions, points beyond vision. In the Empyrean, there is neither space nor matter and, consequently, neither objects nor eyes. The only verifiably realized 'vision' – certainly for the reader, but perhaps for Dante too – is the poem itself.

However, we have also noted that some of the final metaphors suggest that in the end the poem is a forgetting and a scattering of the images it has gathered together. So neither is the poem itself the final object. It directs us to look beyond itself, even though there is no further object that can be seen. This 'visionary' poem is, after all, a relation to what cannot be seen. Seeing and saying operate to 'neutralize' each other, in Blanchot's sense of the neuter – that is, each modality is broken open by its relation with the other to an outside on which it intrinsically depends. Alternatively, we could say that the unsayable is supplemented by vision in a way that makes vision a Derridean 'supplement'[1]: rather than grounding saying, the 'vision' on which saying is supposed to rest opens it to the *in*visible and thus to further references that proliferate without being grounded in any visible presence.

What I wish to underline about language through reference to Blanchot is especially its relation to what cannot be seen or illuminated. This dark side of language showing up only as 'shadowy prefaces' is the *Paradiso*'s ultimate (or, more exactly, penultimate) concern. It cannot be positively described, but is indirectly conveyed through apophatic strategies of the self-undermining of language. Throughout his theoretical writings, Blanchot describes an *un*working of the work, and this is exactly what Dante undertakes in the final movement of his poem. The work must undo itself in order to give place to what is unassimilably beyond it, what Blanchot calls the Outside, *le Dehors*. Opening towards an infinite, indefinable Outside is the gesture that Blanchot sets over against every effort of dialectical thought to return to the Same and affirm the One.

Dante's unworking of the work is symbolized especially by the scattering of Sibyl's leaves and in the Forgetting that overcomes Dante as he consummates his vision. The totality of experience that the poem since its inception has been assiduously gathering and elaborating, with reiterated promises of a complete vision of God *in finis*, bursts apart in the final canto. The poem is consummated not in an all-comprehensive vision but in its own undoing and in a forgetting that effectuate its opening to the dimension of the unrepresentable and invisible. The final gaze looks beyond the poem itself and beyond all its representations. We have images for the final vision of the Trinity and Incarnation, yet they are still only *images* of the invisible God, shadows of inaccessible light, and the deeper meaning of these final representations remains sealed up in what escapes representation altogether.

Such is indeed the very nature of 'images' as Blanchot also understands them. They are the 'duplicity' of revelation, veiling even as they unveil. 'That which veils in revealing, the veil that reveals in re-veiling in the ambiguous indecision of the word revelation, is the image' (*Ce qui voile en révélant, le voile qui révèle en revoilant dans l'indécision ambiguë du mot révéler, c'est l'image*, L'entretien infini, p. 42). In *Purgatorio*

XXX.64–9, on the threshold of the *Paradiso*, the appearance of Beatrice in and practically *as* her veils is a perfect illustration of this, as is also the pageantry and parading in veiled allegorical figures of the books of the Bible in *Purgatorio* XXXII. These final cantos of the *Purgatorio*, in their featuring precisely the veil as the burden of the poem's apocalyptic revelation, form a transition to the radically apophatic mode of the *Paradiso*.

The poem's ultimate fulfillment consists in, or at least passes by way of, the scattering and forgetting of its own representations. However, what is beyond representation altogether is No-thing. What this failure of language opens upon is no object. What Dante sees on the far side of language he understands as divinity, and yet, again, 'no man hath seen God at any time' (I John 4: 12) 'or can see' him (1 Timothy 6:16). To this extent, the 'vision' folds back into the writing – into the language of the poem. But this language itself, since it refers to nothing, has now become No-thing, the neuter – and thereby an Opening to everything: the Infinite. Language that no longer designates anything in particular, nevertheless, *qua* language, signifies the relation of all things without limit, their unlimited potential relatedness, their infinite mutual relations.

Seeing and saying are related through mutual forgetfulness, as Blanchot again divines: 'To see is perhaps to forget to speak, and to speak is to draw from the bottom of the word the forgetting that is the inexhaustible' (*Voir, c'est peut-être oublier de parler, et parler, c'est puiser au fond de la parole l'oubli qui est l'inépuisable*).[2] This mutual neutralization of seeing and saying opens an inexhaustible field of free invention, in fact, an infinite space of the neuter. Dante has pushed the visionary claims of his language to their limit and has exposed this limit at which vision turns out to be grounded on non-vision. Forgetting, as the obliteration of saying and seeing, turns up underneath both forms of experience or representation. Neither exactly visual nor verbal, Dante's revelation becomes uncannily and unclassifiably other and 'divine'. As such, it is infinite, an infinite 'holding between' (entre-tenir), as is also Blanchot's 'infinite conversation' (*entretien infini*).

The non-seeing of the literary work bears decisively on the status of its words. It confers unlimited freedom – there is no longer any constraint imposed by a finite object as limit. Since Dante cannot objectively say what he has experienced, he is untrammelled and free in what he does say about it. And his Saying even becomes absolute, as if it were itself the whole of what it is about. This freedom can, of course, be abused and become a perversion, if it is not accompanied by the countervailing movement of disclaimer that Dante insists on all through the *Paradiso* through his declarations of ineffability.

Blanchot is understandably suspicious of the unlimited powers of a language that is not limited by any object:

> - In this liberty, there is some facileness... Language acts as if we could see the thing from all angles.
> - And the perversion begins then. The world no longer presents itself as a word, but as something seen yet emancipated of the limitations of sight. As not a manner of saying, but a transcendent manner of seeing.
>
> - *Dans cette liberté, il y a de la facilité. Le langage fait comme si nous pouvions voir la chose de tous les côtés.*
> - *Et la perversion commence alors. La parole ne se présente plus comme une parole, mais comme une vue affranchie des limitations de la vue. Non pas une manière de dire, mais une manière transcendante de voir.*
>
> (*L'entretien infini*, p. 40)

This diagnosis describes with striking accuracy an aspect of Dante's use of language. Dante does use language in such a way as to promote it to a transcendent kind of sight, indeed, in the end, to a vision of transcendent Deity. This divine vision is the final goal of the *Divine Comedy* as a whole – hinted at first in *Inferno* (I.112–29) and actually realized progressively in the *Paradiso*. In this last segment of the poem, in subtle and telling ways, Dante turns language as the medium of the poem and its vision into the very object of his vision (as argued in sec. 2 concerning the Heaven of Jove). Language itself at crucial points becomes at least ambiguously transcendent: it is projected and explored as divine Word. Dante thus expresses exemplarily and symbolically the tendency of language to become a 'transcendent manner of seeing' that Blanchot detects as a danger inherent in our discursive culture, with its characteristic conjugation of saying and seeing, ever since its Greek beginnings.

Blanchot understands the word in these terms to be per se 'transgression'. Whereas the look or regard is limited by its object, the word knows no limit. It passes beyond all limits towards the unlimited, the infinite or the 'unlimited of the all'.

> The word is war and madness against the look. The terrible word passes beyond every limit and even the unlimitedness of the all: it takes the thing from where the thing does not take or view nor ever will view itself; it transgresses the laws, frees itself from orientation, disorients.
>
> *La parole est guerre et folie au regard. La terrible parole passe outre à toute limite et même à l'illimité du tout: elle prend la chose par où celle-ci ne se prend pas, ne se voit pas, ne se verra jamais; elle transgresse les lois, s'affranchit de l'orientation, elle désoriente.*
> (*L'entretien infini*, p. 40)

We can hardly deny that Dante's vision ultimately – after the presentation of a perfectly and hierarchically ordered universe, from the bottom of hell to the top of the heavens, both physical and spiritual – is of this order in its disproportion with anything precisely sayable: it explores the unlimitedness of language. It would then be vision in language and in the infinity of the word rather than as delimited by any definable, presentable object. The focus on God would operate metaphorically to heighten the pretensions of language to communicate infinity and totality rather than to delimit language by reference to a circumscribable object.

Of course, Dante does not simply dispense with the visible object: on the contrary, his poem is intensely visual throughout and is sharply aimed at a final vision. In line with the prophetic tradition of the *vates* transmitted by Virgil and cross-fertilized with biblical visionary prophecy in the style of Ezekiel *et al.*, Dante's revelation is emphatically visionary. Nevertheless, his vision is projected from language and ends up without any extra-linguistic object: God cannot be seen as an object in external space. Dante presents rather a transcendental vision *in language* – just as Blanchot suspects. Actually, Saint Augustine, writing in *De Trinitate*, Book XV, of an intellection of the Word that transcends all physical senses, had long before contemplated the peculiar kind of vision of and in the Word beyond visible and audible words that Dante in effect realizes in his *Paradiso*.[3] Seeing *in the word*, so mistrusted by Blanchot, is indeed intrinsic to the hermeneutic tradition of Western humanities as reconstructed notably by Gadamer.[4]

Blanchot is contesting the fundamental orientation of saying to seeing, the assumption that saying is referred to something beyond it and present as an object that could also be immediately seen. This schema is embodied exemplarily by the *Divine Comedy* as a visionary poem, and yet Dante also contrives to dissolve the visual referent as a positive, objective presence: it dissolves into a saying that exceeds all limitations of a definable object. One telling instance is where Dante says that he believes that he saw what he attempts unsuccessfully to describe *because* in saying so he feels his being expand into a larger orbit, evidently a higher degree of freedom and ecstasy:

> *La forma universal di questo nodo*
> *credo ch' i' vidi, perché più di largo,*
> *dicendo questo, mi sento ch' i' godo.*
> (XXXIII. 91–3)
> The universal form of this knot
> I believe I saw, because in saying this,
> I feel that I enjoy more amply.

The 'seeing' to which Dante lays claim is grasped, even by him, rather as a *feeling*; it is projected in desire and delight. This is perhaps a higher sort of 'seeing' than could possibly be remembered or described. It is without a discrete visual object: more than vision, it is 'visionary'.

To this extent, Dante proposes a vision in and through language, which transcends vision in the literal sense. *Visibile parlare* ('visible speech') is a Dantesque theme that lends itself to analysis in terms of the speaking as *not* seeing theorized by Blanchot. In fact, Dante's 'visible speech' in the *Paradiso* seems to be intended as a way of evoking the invisible divinity in a linguistic medium that becomes im-mediate and present without limit. This is how the divine is present in language – *not* as referred, beyond language, to an object other than language itself. The paradox on which Dante plays in seeing letters written in the Heaven of Jove is that writing, the medium of mediation, shows up as an immediate presence of the Name or essence of God.

Whereas Blanchot, in his ongoing polemics against 'dialectics', in principle rejects mediation altogether, Dante's universe is through and through analogical – a mediation between finite and infinite, between human and divine. It is a gift of grace from a loving and all-powerful Creator. Blanchot no longer believes in this metaphysical vision. In this regard, the sense of transgression is ultimately very different for Dante and even the opposite of what it is for Blanchot. Yet formally their discoveries in journeying to the limits of language and peering beyond are strikingly parallel and—analogous! In putting it that way, of course, I am seeing more through Dante's eyes than Blanchot's. Blanchot rejects the analogical understanding of reality as based on the analogy of being (*analogia entis*), and this determines his orientation as fundamentally different from Dante's.[5] Still, we have everything to learn from him about the structure of transcendence inherent in language as it bears upon Dante's experience of the limits of language. The radical divergence in underlying metaphysical assumptions makes the comparison only the more revealing.

For Blanchot, a visual object posits a distancing from what is known; it implies a totalizing gaze that unifies what it sees in the form of an object: every view is a view of the whole (*toute vue est vue d'ensemble*). 'Seeing', Blanchot writes, 'makes use of separation not as mediator but as a means of immediacy, as im-mediator' (*Voir, c'est se servir de la séparation, non pas comme médiatrice, mais comme un moyen d'immédiation, comme im-médiatrice,* L'entretien infini, p. 39). As such, seeing is essentially experience of continuity and celebrates the sun, which is to say the One – the unifying principle of all, the emanating source of light and energy (p. 39). Speech, in contrast, has no definite object or discrete, free-standing units, but opens infinitely in the direction of an Other – a potential partner in conversation. Blanchot proposes this 'infinite conversation' as an alternative model to the dominant Western epistemology, which has been based on sight ever since Plato's divided line leading up to the direct vision of the Forms or Essences of all reality. In Blanchot's 'view'

> Speaking is not seeing. Speaking liberates thought of the optical exigency which, in Western tradition for millennia, dominates our approach to things and induces us to think under the guarantee of light or of the absence of light.
>
> *Parler, ce n'est pas voir. Parler libère la pensée de cette exigence optique qui, dans la tradition occidentale, soumet depuis des millénaires notre approche des choses et nous invite à penser sous la garantie de la lumière ou de l'absence de lumière.* (*L'entretien infini*, p. 38)

Blanchot recognizes the extraordinary power of the word when freed from the limits of sight, and he fears this freedom's being recast as still a kind of vision, yet vision made absolute. This is a temptation especially for literature. By the privileged power of the word,

> [t]he novelist lifts the roofs and delivers his personage to a penetrating gaze. His mistake is to take language still for vision, but absolute vision.
>
> *Le romancier soulève les toits et livre son personnage au regard pénétrant. Son tort est de prendre le langage pour une vision encore, mais absolue.* (*L'entretien infini*, p. 40)

Speaking, in effect, according to Blanchot, far from simply supplanting vision, absolutizes it: speech carries vision to infinity. This is, in effect, to contemplate the invisibility of things. However, it is to see *nothing* – no thing.[6] And such a word, one that sees nothing, is no longer referred to a thing: it is blind, without visible content, but it is also an open word, open to everything.[7]

Such absolutization of language is dangerous precisely as posing a threat of idolatry. Blanchot's critique coincides with a theological critique that has been renewed again and again over centuries. Originally the danger was that of forsaking the God beyond representation, the God transcending the world and every image.[8] However, Dante also relinquishes the images he has constructed and obliterates his vision in Forgetting: he indicates the dispersion and forgetting of his whole vision in its consummation at the poem's end. Although he uses intensively the metaphor of an infinite and divinizing 'vision', he also points out its limits and remains, even at the height of his vision in the presence of God, cognizant of being in relation to the absolutely Unknowable that outstrips all analogical approaches that have been graciously granted.

Thus, Dante's absolutized vision is not an idol but an icon – it does still refer beyond itself, even beyond the break of the semiological relation of denotative reference: it is a thing allegorically signifying a higher reality, even though it gives no possible knowledge or scientific definition of the divinity towards which it is directed. Analogy in the Dionysian tradition that Dante follows has this effect of opening to the Infinite.[9]

Blanchot discovers language as not limited from without, but as absolute and as having all of its limits or determinations immanently within itself. Language thereby transcends its status as referential, as referred to something else. Sight, by contrast, is referred to what it 'sees' at a distance from itself and what therefore delimits it. This infinity of language in its immanence and as not delimited from outside itself has also been rediscovered in various ways by modern linguists from Humboldt through Saussure to Sapir and Benveniste. For Blanchot, it gives language a quality of infinity that he wants not to confuse with sight, which is limited by its object.

Dante discovers the same properties of language as in itself infinite or as unlimited by anything that it does not take into itself and shape, and yet he does not eschew the metaphorics of sight for the experience he accedes to through language. Indeed after its implosion, faced with the impossibility of representation, language is only a relation and in some sense a non-relation to the experience to which it alludes. It is but a failing to relate in the sense of representation. What Dante *says* is a testimonial to his experience – or rather to the feeling it has left distilled into his heart (XXXIII.60–3).

Dante evidently does make a claim to absolute vision attained or at least conveyed through language in his poem. Yet we have brought to focus how he also shatters that claim at the climax of his vision – which is achieved precisely in its break-down and failure. Dante thus recapitulates the scopocentrism that characterizes Western metaphysical culture from Plato through Hegel, but he also stages its collapse and looks – or rather steps – beyond it. He thereby steps into the precincts of 'the sacred' as it is construed by Blanchot.

Blanchot (in the wake of Hölderlin) describes a 'double infidelity', whereby gods and humans both withdraw from one another. He describes a sacred poetry that arises in this 'dehiscence' between the two spheres. Dante is, of course, far from such perspectives, especially when they are developed in pagan and ultimately atheistic directions, but in the end Dante's efforts to enact the divine vision are realized likewise through withdrawal and rupture. Rather than mediating everything by his speech, he is placed before the im-mediate, where speech breaks off. This cutting off from totality as constructed by language is what Blanchot calls the sacred: 'this empty and pure space that distinguishes the spheres [of gods and mortals], there is *the sacred*, the intimacy of the tearing that is the sacred' (*ce lieu vide et pur qui distingue les sphères, c'est là le sacré, l'intimité de la déchirure qu'est le sacré*).[10]

Dante builds into his great synthetic work this tearing asunder, this counter-movement of drawing away and of dwelling in separation, in the bridgeless gulf that yawns between him and the would-be object of his experience. These are features of his poem that have become more difficult to overlook and underestimate, thanks to the apophatic turn of postmodern culture.[11]

With the prominent metaphysical assumptions of a more dogmatic age, such as both Dante and thinkers of difference react against in their respective eras and intellectual milieus, these negative features of the sacred that are most manifest in emptiness and loss tend to be effaced altogether. Rather than appearing simply as admitted limits that Dante has to somehow finesse or get around in pursuit of his quest, we come much closer to understanding that it is precisely in and by these 'impediments' that Dante's quest is constituted and is carried to its highest degree of accomplishment.

For Blanchot, as much as for Dante, art has its origin in the ungraspable that is the sacred:

> Why such an intimate alliance between art and the sacred? Because in the movement in which art, the sacred, that which shows itself, that which conceals itself, manifestation and dissimulation change places unceasingly, call to each other and seize each other there where, nevertheless, they do not fulfil themselves except as the approach of the ungraspable, the work finds the deep reserve of which it has need: hidden and preserved by the presence of the god, manifest and apparent by the obscurity and the distance that constitutes its space and that it arouses, as if to come to the light of day. This is the holding back that then allows it to address itself to the world even while reserving itself, to be the always reserved beginning of every history.

> *Pourquoi l'alliance si intime de l'art et du sacré? C'est que, dans le mouvement où l'art, le sacré, ce qui se montre, ce qui se dérobe, l'évidence et la dissimulation s'échangent sans arrêt, s'appellent et se saisissant là où pourtant ils ne s'accomplissent que comme l'approche de l'insaisissable, l'œuvre trouve la profonde réserve dont elle a besoin: cachée et préservée par la présence du dieu, manifeste et apparente par l'obscurité et ce lointain qui constitue son espace et qu'elle suscite comme pour venir au jour. C'est cette réserve qui lui permet alors de s'adresser au monde tout en se réservant, d'être le commencement toujours réservé de toute histoire.* (L'espace littéraire, pp. 310–11)

A space of separation from the ultimate defines the 'space of literature' for Blanchot, and it is also the space for Dante's explorations of the 'impossible' vision of God in the poetry of the *Paradiso*.

An issue that arises in comparing Dante with Blanchot is that of whether the sacred or the divine vision actually 'takes place' or not. For Blanchot, it is 'the impossible' and always *in*actual, and yet his own writing is centrally about this non-event at the origin of the work of art. Dante, in contrast, seems to be insisting on an actual event having occurred as the condition rendering his poem possible. At the same time, the poem testifies relentlessly to the *im*possibility of actually presenting, by remembering and describing, what it is all, nevertheless, obsessively about. In the end, his poem offers an experience of language. Poetic experience of language at its limits perhaps in some sense *is* the experience of divinity and of Paradise as presented by Dante's poem. And here a similar 'indiscretion' or collapsing together of experience and language can be signalled as characterizing Blanchot's novels (*Thomas l'obscur, Aminadab* and *Le Très-Haut*). In them, 'the language of experience is nothing other than the experience of language'.[12]

Blanchot describes, moreover, the curiously 'comic' condition of the writer in terms that perfectly fit Dante's situation of writing about nothing (that can be said or written about) at the apex of his *Comedy*:

> The writer finds himself in the more and more comic condition of having nothing to write, of having no means of writing it, and of being constrained by an extreme necessity to continue to write it. Having nothing to express must be taken in the simplest sense. Whatever he may say, it is nothing. The world, things, knowledge are for him nothing but reference points in the emptiness. And he is himself already reduced to nothing. Nothing is his material. He rejects the forms by which it offers itself to him as being something.... the 'I have nothing to say' of the writer, like that of the accused, encloses the whole secret of his condition.
>
> *L'écrivain se trouve dans cette condition de plus en plus comique de n'avoir rien à écrire, de n'avoir aucun moyen de l'écrire et d'être*

> *contraint par une nécessité extrême de toujours l'écrire. N'avoir rien à exprimer doit être pris dans le sens le plus simple. Quoi qu'il veuille dire, ce n'est rien. Le monde, les choses, le savoir ne lui sont que des points de repère à travers le vide. Et lui-même est déjà réduit à rien. Le rien est sa matière. Il rejette les formes par lesquelles elle s'offre à lui comme étant quelque chose.... le 'Je n'ai rien à dire' de l'écrivain, comme celui de l'accusé, enferme tout le secret de sa condition solitaire.*[13]

How amusing that Blanchot should characterize this condition of the writer as 'comic'. This word has something of the cosmic disproportion in his discourse that it has also in Dante's use of it for the title of his poem. While Blanchot describes the objectless vision that takes itself for object as a tragedy, Dante turns it into 'comedy' because for Dante this Nothing (nothing that can be grasped or said) is God rather than just emptiness and abandon. There is thus a marked difference in mood between the vision of Dante and the limit-experience of Blanchot, and I have already suggested that an analogical metaphysical view of the universe as revealing somehow a transcendent source underlies this difference.[14] However, structurally the experiences are the same: both are experience of the limits of experience and take place in and through writing.

Blanchot, in his analyses of the undoing of the work (*désœuvrement*) and its reduction to no-thing, is thinking of the literary work in general, but Dante's *Comedy*, especially in its final movement in the *Paradiso*, illustrates his theory perhaps better than any other literary work. To see this, we must suspend our taking the vision positively as a seen correlative, free-standing and independent of the writing, and accept that the writing *is*, in a crucial sense, the vision, and that Dante's uncanny writing opens blindly to the Outside as what it cannot see or describe. This Outside is experienced as non-experience or as the beyond of experience: Dante says from the third tercet of the third canticle (*Par.* I.4–9) that his mind is not able to gather in the realm he has visited – or the dimension of absolute language and ultimate reality that he has been given to fathom. In this regard, Dante's writing is like Blanchot's – an infinite conversation on the impossible. Of course, Dante understands his experience theologically as an approach to God. But this Name finally relinquishes all conceptually definable content. What Dante is able to deliver of this non-experience is given rather through the *un*doing of his work – so that it remains gaping open in the direction of this divinity that it cannot grasp.

The *un*working of the work actually works in tandem with the opposite movement in which the work constructs a vision through language – what the *Comedy*, of course, *also* is par excellence. But we have seen that this work of construction in language is reversed in the end and opens itself to what is beyond language – particularly through the allusion to the scattering of the leaves of Sibyl and in the forgetting that underlies remembering. The work of words serves to open upon a wordless dimension that underlies it throughout the whole poem and across history and all experience, as we are made to realize retrospectively. Dante's work, in the ultimate moment in which it could be expected to achieve completion, is reversed into unworking and rather points to something altogether beyond the compass of its representative capacities – the 'vision' of 'God'.

For Blanchot, literary works are 'incomplete and as if open, the passage which is now the only essential work' (*inachevés et comme ouverts, le passage qui est maintenant la seule œuvre essentielle*, L'entretien infini, p. 319). And precisely this is paradigmatically the case with Dante's *Paradiso*: it perfectly embodies and enacts Blanchot's prescriptions for the original experience of literature. Yet Blanchot seems not to have realized this. He, too, was conditioned to see Dante in a way excluding the kind of insight that his own thought has done so much to uncover and that aids us to read what he calls 'the most profound question' as already operative in Dante. This is the question which even the question of all (or of everything) – 'la question de tout' – does not comprehend. It remains unavowable as the question that evades all formulas in which it could be asked.[15]

Addendum on analogy

Blanchot assumes that analogy necessarily serves for tying the universe back together into one, whereas the reality he experiences is in the irrevocable entropic dissolution of the 'disaster'.[16] However, analogy also serves to point out infinite difference – precisely that which exists between God and creatures. The Dionysian tradition, within which Dante works, insists on this *disanalogy* at the base of every analogy. In fact, Dionysius the Areopagite is at the origin of a vast theological tradition on analogy in which the Infinite erupts into the finite by 'transgressing towards the mystery that is the rapturous transport of the beauty that saves' (*quel trasgredire verso il mistero che è il rapimento della bellezza che salva*).[17]

In this form, Christianity emphasizes precisely the *transgressiveness* of the relation between the finite and the Infinite. The Word incarnate counts as a transgressor – indeed he is crucified as such. The analogy between visible and invisible beauty consists not just in harmonious proportions but also in rupture and even in scandalous transgression, according to the heirs of this tradition leading directly to Dante. It is picked up by Hans Urs von Balthasar in his emphasis on Christ's paradoxically abject "glory" (*Herrlichkeit*) and again in postmodern times by numerous theological thinkers, including Bruno Forte, within the Augustinian-Thomistic tradition into which Dionysius had been thoroughly integrated:

> In the Word made flesh, Thomas recognizes the eruption of the Other, the appearing of Silence in the Word up to the supreme cry of the ninth hour, the ecstasy of the living God in love with His creature. And it is thus that he intuits that there must be another relation between the Whole and the fragment than the Greek one – rethought by Augustine in Christian terms – of proportion and form, a relation of rupture, of scandal, of transgression.
>
> *Nel Verbo fatto carne Tommaso riconosce l'irruzione dell'Altro, l'affacciarsi del Silenzio nella Parola fino al supremo grido dell'ora nona, l'estasi del Dio vivente innamorato della Sua creatura. Ed è*

così che egli intuisce che deve esistere un altro rapporto fra il Tutto e il frammento, oltre quello 'greco' - ripensato cristianamente da Agostino - della proporzione e della forma, un rapporto di rottura, di scandalo, di trasgressione. (Forte, p. 33)

Forte describes the relation of analogy, articulated as a conjugation of proportionate analogy (between two relations) and attributive analogy (through mutual participation in a 'unicum'), as aimed, beyond form and harmony, at splendor and transcendence – at 'transgression' (*trasgressione*). Both forms of analogy are governed by a tension towards transgression, and as such analogy is 'turned toward transgressing the unsayable in obedience to God's saying himself in the creation and in His historical revelation' (*volta a trasgredire l'indicibile in obbedienza al dirsi di Dio nella creazione e nella Sua rivelazione storica*, p. 30).

8

Writing – The 'Essential Experience'

Dante insists that he cannot describe his experience of approaching the direct vision of God. In fact, there are no concepts which are adequate to God, as the tradition of negative theology concordantly attests. Dante's approach proceeds rather by approximation to a degree zero of writing. That is to say, Dante enters progressively into an experience of the absolute through progressively relinquishing all linguistic grasp and conceptual definition of himself and his world and, most specifically, of their presumable necessary Ground. This is comparable to Blanchot's radical pursuit of writing as a process of neutering all being, of 'experiencing' being as nothing, or as stripped of all the delimitations and qualifications shrouded in which it is normally presented to us. Blanchot's approach to this limit-experience, just like Dante's, is through the experience of writing.

Both Dante and Blanchot discover absolute 'being' as 'the obscure' through their asymptotic approach to the 'space of literature'. They have different religious ideas and convictions, but both must ultimately relinquish all their *a priori* notions in pursuing the experience of writing all the way to the limit at which nothing remains that is not utterly unhinged from the known order of beings and from our customary conceptual structures. We approach the groundless ground of all through utter surrender to the remaking of the world in the obscurity of writing. For Dante, this immersion in absolute obscurity is the mystical encounter with God, whereas Blanchot interprets it atheistically as an 'inner experience' along the lines suggested by Georges Bataille. But these divergent interpretations reflect the different cultural bearings of Blanchot and Dante without effacing the intrinsic similarities in their respective experiences of the absolute made possible by its relation to the space of literature.

The 'essential experience', in Blanchot's idiom, is not 'of' anything because it is experience of everything and of being as absolute – which is not 'being' or anything else that can be said or even 'be' in a graspable sense. This is fundamentally the experience that has been described or rather pursued through discarding all description and acknowledging its impossibility in the tradition of negative theology. Blanchot, of course, does not want to embrace theology of any order, however negative it may be, even though his 'conversation' with it is unending. And yet the seminal force of negative theology in his *oeuvre* registers nevertheless – particularly in the voice of others.

In a section of *L'entretien infini* entitled 'How to discover the obscure?' Blanchot quotes a passage from Ives Bonnefoy that makes explicit the link between poetry at its limit and negative theology (poetic figuration transforming theological impossibility to improbability):

> *I dedicate this book to the improbable, which is to say, to that which is. To a spirit of wakefulness. To negative theologies. To a desired poetry of rains, of waiting and of wind. To a great realism, which aggravates rather than resolving, which designates the obscure, which takes illuminations for clouds which are always capable of being ripped apart. Which strive for a high and impracticable clarity.*
>
> Je dédie ce livre à l'improbable, c'est-à-dire à ce qui est. A un esprit de veille. Aux théologies négatives. A une poésie désirée, de pluies, d'attente et de vent. A un grand réalisme, qui aggrave au lieu de résoudre, qui désigne l'obscur, qui tienne les clartés pour nuées toujours déchirables. Qui ait souci d'une haute et impraticable clarté. (p. 58)

Negative theology is presented here not only through explicit nomination but also through imagery specifically in the Dionysian tradition of the cloud of unknowing. As discovered by Dionysius the Areopagite, the fountainhead of Christian negative theology celebrated by Dante in *Paradiso* XXVIII.130–32, God is experienced in a cloud of luminous darkness.[1] Likewise, ultimate reality can be present to finite consciousness in poetry only as the obscure. The absolute light and clarity of what is most real can for us be but clouds, which, however, are always susceptible to being torn open, thus exposing the real that we are always awaiting and pining for. The real – as also with the Lacanian homonym (*le réel*) – can neither be definitively alienated and sealed off into the impossible nor be fit into our order of possibilities. As the real which is, it is rather the 'improbable' – the reality that cannot quite be accounted for in discourse. Hence the approach to it can proceed only by means of an undoing of discourse. This type of apophatic procedure defines a kind of poetry that could be traced from Dante to Bonnefoy, in whom Blanchot recognizes it for what it is. Such poetry serves for the reinvention of new hope that, paradoxically, gives us what in fact is. It gives us what actually is in the form of 'the improbable'.

We can recognize in Dante's *Paradiso* the most compelling case of the essential experience of literature that Blanchot likewise explores. Whereas Blanchot thinks of this as a particularly modern experience that he traces from Hölderlin and Mallarmé to Rilke, Char and Bonnefoy, its more original discovery is in Dante – as is also the case with so much of what has come to characterize modern and especially postmodern experience. Making this connection foregrounds the theological roots of our own culture.

Blanchot's theological poet of preference is Hölderlin, and it is especially as negative theological poet that Blanchot privileges him – as the poet of the absence or defecting or default of God (*Gottes Fehl*). In later Hölderlin, according to Blanchot, the task of the poet is to stand before the absence of God. Whereas previously, in Greece, it was in the gods' overwhelming presence that poets were called to stand, so as to mediate the divine energy to humanity, today, in the modern West, it is of the absence of the gods that the poet is called to be the mediator and witness. He is called even to a double infidelity, reproducing that by which the gods have deserted humanity in modern times. The gods must be remembered precisely as turning away. The poet must preserve their infidelity by 'forgetting all': 'It is the divine infidelity that [the poetic word] must contain, preserve; it is 'under the form of infidelity where there is forgetting of all' (*c'est l'infidélité divine qu'il doit contenir, preserver, c'est 'sous la forme de l'infidélité où il y a oubli de tout'*, L'espace littéraire, p. 370). Only so will the poet enter into 'communication with the god who turns away' (*communication avec le dieu qui se détourne*, p. 370).

The essential experience described by Blanchot as 'writing' is an experience not of self-realization or of active creation but rather of becoming an articulation of an event that one does not control or comprehend. It is in passivity and *un*working (*désoeuvrement*), in being exposed to the night, that the writer attains to this ultimate experience. Dante has such an experience in his approach to what he understands as the divine vision. Being completely disarmed and losing mastery are the hallmarks of the ascent as Dante describes it. It is not anything that he can deliberately do – he cannot even describe it. It is what happens to him beyond his control in the night of a mystic encounter – what is, in effect, a luminous cloud of unknowing.

Dante's analysis of being wrought upon and overwhelmed in the event of inspiration is comparable to what Blanchot describes as the essential experience of the poet, paradigmatically Orpheus. It is an experience of writing because in writing one begins the world over again on the basis of nothing. Nothing is given for writing, as Blanchot conceives it, at least not as fixed in form prior to the writing itself: writing cuts from nowhere into nothing. Etymologically 'writ' or 'script' is rooted in cutting and carving. One cuts against every existing order of things in order to let things appear in their emergence from the abyss of namelessness and wordlessness.

In Blanchot's conception, the act of writing, as an original cut from nowhere into nothing, sets aside all *a priori* orders of the world. The act of writing or of digging out verses (*creuser les vers*) requires 'renouncing every idol' and 'breaking with everything' that is (*Qui creuse le vers doit renoncer à toute idole, doit briser avec tout*, L'espace littéraire, p. 38). This is essentially what negative theology also does in relinquishing all concepts of God as idolatrous. Blanchot describes it as an escape from Being as certitude and an encounter with the absence of the gods (*Qui creuse le vers, échappe à l'être comme certitude, rencontre l'absence des dieux*, p. 37). Writing, so conceived, is not essentially an expression of oneself or one's own ideas, which would inevitably be achieved in relation to the given order of the world as one perceives and lives it. All *that* is annihilated in writing: one surrenders oneself to an emergence from nowhere and becomes passive – or rather a receptive agent. Writing is the creative act from which the world originates – as in the work of art, according to Heidegger's *Der Ursprung des Kunstwerks* ('The Origin of the Work of Art'), however, with all pretension to being a creator, or even an autonomous agent, removed. Blanchot's writer is given over essentially to suicide – as modelled by Mallarmé's *Igitur*.

These are not, of course, recognizably the terms of Dante's portrayal of writing in the *Paradiso*, and yet essentially writing in the *Paradiso* is for Dante an unselfing or a transcending of self (a *mors mistica*), a yielding to 'inspiration', in which he is invaded by nothing he can properly conceive or say (see Appendix). He is released into what he cannot know. He too enters into a night or cloud of unknowing in order to accomplish the ultimate writerly act of *unworking*. The whole of being is at stake here, and it happens in language, in the language of being, but even more directly in the being of language as it is played out in the poem. The discovery of the space of literature as the essential experience, whether this leads to a proclaimed revelation of truth or to an experience beyond the possibility of truth (and of discourse *tout court*), is shared in common by Blanchot and Dante. At least it is described by each in terms that are mutually illuminating.

For Blanchot, the night in which one writes is the endless night of the death of God proclaimed by Nietzsche's madman (*Der tolle Mensch*) as suspending us in endless nothing (*ein unendliche Nichts*, *The Gay Science*, sec.125). Dante's blindness, to the contrary, is the luminous darkness spoken of in the tradition of Dionysius: it is the unknowing into which he is constrained to enter as he approaches the blinding light of God.

Dante and Blanchot both enter into the act of writing as prior to any order of the world. All *a prioris* vanish and dissolve into the night of writing, which is not even an act so much as a passion. God is dead, say Nietzsche and his heirs. God is inconceivable, say negative theologians. Writers like Dante and Blanchot find in this act of abandon to passivity the essential solitude that takes them to the origin of the whole order of things in a namelessness that can be conceived of only as an abyss. It is by receding into writing rather than by transcending it into any independently known order of things or into an externally graspable object that Dante and Blanchot alike approach the absolute. They have different conceptions of this absolute, but both acknowledge its 'impossibility' or ultimate inconceivability. For Dante, it is negative theology that illuminates this predicament, whereas for Blanchot it is rather a negation of theology. Yet all their affirmations are in either case retracted. Blanchot disqualifies negation by the neuter, while Dante mediates theological doctrine by poetry. Both decisively neuter the potency of their respective discourses to make positive affirmations.

Rather than using words to express thoughts and to move through them towards things, writing consists radically in entering into words in their emergence from being, from the dark abyss of the inconceivable. This is writing both for Blanchot and for Dante. Their experience of writing is one not of using words as tools to express their thoughts or to grasp things as they presumably are in the order of the world, which is the order of the word. Rather, writing at this level enters into words and reaches down to their origin in being. This experience requires of the artists an *un*working of their works and activity as writers. They must sacrifice their own work in order to sink themselves into its inspiration. This requires a kind of intense passivity or rather receptivity. It has been described by poets like Keats as 'negative capability'. It is also familiar to the experience of many mystics. John of the Cross's *noche oscura* embraces both registers, as does Dante's 'paradiso'. Whereas Blanchot finds there the neuter, Dante finds God.

The neuter is being without qualification, which is exactly how God is understood in classical negative theology from Dionysius and Eriugena to Aquinas and Eckhart. Even the qualification of 'being' in any sense we can grasp must be removed recursively from what can only be described as 'neither/nor'. The neuter cannot be given an adequate definition any more than God can. It can be defined rather functionally – by how the word is used – particularly in order to back away from the definite A or not-A type of meaning of any concept.

As Blanchot writes, the neuter is simply the naked being of the word, the 'unworked word': 'that which approaches is the neutral word, indistinct, which is the being of the word, the word unworked of which nothing can be made' (*ce qui s'approche, c'est cette parole neutre, indistincte, qui est l'être de la parole, la parole désœuvrée dont il ne peut rien être fait,* L'espace littéraire, p. 240). In this word, language is 'the unavailable' (*l'indisponible*) and 'the pure indeterminate' (*le langage est le pur indéterminé*, p. 240).

9

The Gaze of Orpheus

Blanchot sounds the unfathomable relations between the author, the work and its 'inspiration' in terms that invite comparison to Dante's writing of his work and its relation to Beatrice or to 'God' – or to an even deeper, unknowable source of inspiration than any theological concept or amorous construct can express. 'The Gaze of Orpheus' (*Le regard d'Orphée*) is the title of the section of *L'espace littéraire* towards which the whole book is directed, according to a prefatory 'Note' (p. 8). In this section, Blanchot writes of a profoundly obscure 'point' towards which Orpheus descends, but he is not allowed to gaze on it directly. His *work* is to lead the invisible beauty of this 'point', which inspires him, to the daylight, where he can give it visible form and figure. Everything is permitted him, 'except to look at this point directly, to look at the center of the night in the night' (*Orphée peut tout, sauf regarder ce 'point' en face, sauf regarder le centre de la nuit dans la nuit*, p. 225). He must turn away from this unfathomable night in order to be able to approach it, attract it to himself and conduct it to the light of day. However, in his actual approach, Orpheus forgets his (artistic) work and forgets it necessarily, since his highest exigency is not to create the work but to behold this point and apprehend its essence 'in the heart of the night' (*au coeur de la nuit*), where alone it is essential.

For Dante, the vision of God, and not the work that he produces as a result, is likewise his ultimate end and purpose. Aesthetic production of the poem is in principle a by-product of a spiritual journey in response to a summons from God. Just as for Orpheus, so for Dante, his work is secondary to his quest for a vision of the invisible. By turning to Eurydice, against the divine interdiction, Orpheus abandons and ruins his work. He sacrifices the work to his passion for Eurydice, for he desires not the daylight image of her but her deep, unfathomable being in the dark of night. This is his infinite passion, and it is greater than any desire, however great, to accomplish his work. Dante likewise has to forsake his work in the end for the abyss of the divine that determines his desire as an overwhelming, all-transcending drive. All else must be left behind as he is absorbed by this consuming passion for what cannot be experienced to the end without sacrificing all.

Orpheus's quest is explicitly for a transgressive vision. He disobeys the god's express command not to look at his love until he has returned from the underworld to the daylight world above. He must do so in order to be faithful to his desire to see Eurydice not in her quotidian radiance and truth but in her nocturnal obscurity – when she is invisible, in the 'presence of her infinite absence' (*présence de son absence infinie*, p. 227). In thus sacrificing himself, or in giving himself up to this desire and quest, he is in a sense as dead as she: he no longer lives except for this vision of the dead, in which he dies without end (p. 227).

Orpheus's faithfulness to his passion is 'just', even if it is transgressive. He sacrifices himself to it, accepts his own infinite sojourn in death together with the loss of Eurydice and his own dispersion – his dismemberment and bodily scattering by the fury of the Maenads. All this is necessary to his song as a work of eternal *unworking*. In his very disobedience or transgression, Orpheus opts to obey the deeper exigency that inspires his work (*obéir à l'exigence profonde de l'oeuvre*, p. 228). Beholding Eurydice – without care for his own song – is his inspiration. But this inspiration can become known and celebrated only through Orpheus's and his work's *failure* (*echec*). He has to forget his work, drawn on by the desire that comes from the night. This very failure is intrinsic to and the source of his authenticity (p. 229). By obeying his inspiration, he in fact wins from hell the shadow of infinite absence and conducts it to the daylight of the work.

Orpheus's experience parallels Dante's claims concerning the creation of his poem in the shadow of his experience of Paradise. Dante, too, develops a poetics of failure in order not so much to deliver his final vision as to describe the impediments to his doing so. Paradoxically, the tale of his failure becomes his success, and he too sojourns indefinitely among the dead in the poem which survives him.

What Blanchot says of Orpheus's 'regard' as symbol of the ultimate quest of literature applies equally to Dante's poetic quest for divine vision in the *Paradiso*:

> In this regard, the work is lost. It is the only movement in which it loses itself completely, where something more important than the work, more denuded of importance than the work, announces and affirms itself. The work is everything for Orpheus—except for this regard in which it loses itself, in such manner that it is also only in the regard that it can surpass itself, unite with its origin and consecrate itself in the impossibility.
>
> *En ce regard, l'œuvre est perdue. C'est le seul moment où elle se perd absolument, où quelque chose de plus important que l'œuvre, de plus dénué d'importance qu'elle, s'annonce et s'affirme. L'œuvre est tout pour Orphée, à l'exception de ce regard désiré où elle se perd, de sorte que c'est aussi seulement dans ce regard qu'elle peut se dépasser, s'unir à son origine et se consacrer dans l'impossibilité.* (*L'espace littéraire*, pp. 229–30)

Such is the lesson of Blanchot's Orpheus. And far from serving to distance Dante into the pre-history of outmoded poetic traditions, it rather serves to place Dante's pursuit in the *Paradiso* in the crucible of the essential experience of literature as it has been (re)discovered by Blanchot in modern and contemporary authors. As in Orpheus's quest, so in Dante's, desire is impatient to possess the source of inspiration itself, the origin of the work, to which, however, the work itself must, in the end, be sacrificed.

Dante's ambitions drive him past the project of producing a perfect work. He is attracted most powerfully by what no work can contain: his *Paradiso* is finally a colossal monument to 'the absence of the work'. This is expressed conclusively in the gestures of scattering and forgetting at the end of his poem and journey. This is what makes him a 'writer' in the sense defined by Blanchot and operative again in especially high doses throughout contemporary criticism. 'Writing does not have its end and purpose in the work. In writing the work, we are under the force of attraction of the absence of the work' (*Écrire n'a pas sa fin dans le livre ou dans l'œuvre. Ecrivant l'œuvre, nous sommes sous l'attrait de l'absence d'œuvre*, p. 624). For Dante, as for Meister Eckhart, this is the desire for God. It is finally *God's own desire* and entails losing oneself in the consummation of this desire, in which the ego is consumed.

For Blanchot, this is experience of the neuter and it cannot be of 'God', but this is because of his inadequate understanding of negative theology, which brings out of theology what seems to be its opposite, as long as theology is identified with dogmatic assertion rather than with search and with the most radical negation of any sufficiency that might be claimed for whatever human formula for the holy or whatever human apprehension of the transcendent. Blanchot stresses that the neuter is not merely passive and not merely negative. It is rather proactive and prevenient: its impossible power has always already preceded whatever we can accomplish. These terms could equally describe God and his prevenient grace. Blanchot argues that the neuter is not a transcendental unknown, not the '"absolutely unknowable" subject of pure transcendence, refusing in every way to be known and to express itself' (*'l'absolument inconnaissabile', sujet de pure transcendance, se refusant à toute manière de connaître et de s'exprimer*), but must be found in the tension of what is neither known nor unknown.¹ And likewise the God of negative theology is not an abstract Unknown in a remote transcendence but the unknown in what is most immanent and even incarnate in and among us.²

This absence of the work paradoxically articulates itself more and more in proportion with the ambitiousness of the work. Blanchot observes that, 'The more the Work grows in significance and ambition, containing in itself not only all forms and all powers of discourse, the more the absence of the work seems ready to present itself, yet without ever letting itself be designated' (*Plus l'Œuvre prend de sens et d'ambition, retenant en elle non seulement toutes les œuvres, mais toutes les formes et tous les pouvoirs du discours, plus l'absence d'œuvre semble près de se proposer, sans toutefois jamais se laisser designer, L'entretien infini*, p. 622). Dante's work is as ambitious as they come, and it stands to reason that his final vision should be characterized by a colossal *absence of the work*. Dante makes everything in the *Paradiso* point to what is absent from it. The absence of the work is what, in the end, signifies the vision of God. Dante's work is ever so present in its rhetorical colour and animation, and yet it completes itself by deferring to a Truth which it cannot make present, but which alone can make it complete.

Orpheus loses his work in the desiring gaze. The work is everything to him – *except* for this gaze, in which it is completely lost. The gaze exceeds the work and unites with the work's origin, its reason for being, which is otherwise impossible for the work to attain. The gaze is Orpheus's gift to his work and, at the same time, his sacrifice of it for the infinite desire of its origin. Orpheus embraces the certainty of his failure for the uncertainty of the origin, and the work itself becomes uncertain. The work may even become as if it never were at all. Since all certifiable value is only inner-worldly and requires an order of significances, even the most brilliant masterpiece can become uncertain in its aesthetic value. The gaze of Orpheus breaks all laws and exceeds all limits; it exits from all orders and systems and liberates him from himself and from everything else, everything that is anything within the order of the world (*L'espace littéraire*, p. 231). Similarly Dante, with Christ, might say that he has overcome the world.

And yet Dante discovers that the sense of this overcoming cannot finally be determined as success or victory. The sense of transgression for Dante in the end escapes from sense; it is a total stranger to every rule; it reaches into what Blanchot calls 'the absence of the book', the suspension of every code and system. According to Blanchot, writing is '(pure) exteriority, a stranger to every relation of presence as also to every legality' [*L'écriture, (pure) extériorité, étrangère à toute relation de présence, comme à toute légalité*, 'L'absence de livre', *L'entretien infini*, p. 632].

In order to be faithful to the dark, unnameable source of inspiration of his work, the artist must transgress against the very conditions that make it humanly possible. Finally, the work 'demands a sacrifice of the one who renders it possible' (*l'œuvre . . . demande à celui qui la rend possible un sacrifice*, L'espace littéraire, p. 316). The poet risks being cursed for its sake. Dante, nevertheless, manages to carry out his limit-experience of transgressing and yet to avoid becoming a *poète maudit*. Apparently, he is saved by grace in such a way that, even in transgressing all formulable laws of language and creatureliness, he does not finally violate the deeply divine moral order of the universe beyond all formulable order.

Against the presumptive charge of transgression, which dogs him throughout the journey, as is pointed up particularly by the Ulysses motif, Dante mounts from the beginning of his poem a vast apparatus of legitimization, reaching from God himself down through a relay of blessed ladies, who bid Dante to undertake the journey. The authenticating chain moves back up from Virgil and Beatrice through Saint Bernard to the Virgin Mary and her intercession with God on high at the poem's end. And yet the transgression involved in the artistic logic of the endeavour is made only the more conspicuous: Dante shrinks from transgressing no explicit limit.

The artwork is a by-product of the limit-experience of the Absolute, which is necessarily a transgressive experience and, above all, not one that should be divulged. Paul's experience, as recorded in 2 Corinthians 12, of being rapt into the third heaven and hearing such things as it is not lawful for a man to utter is paradigmatic and is alluded to by Dante from the outset of the *Paradiso* (I.7–9, 70–5). Such is the model of transgression that Dante presents just as lucidly as Blanchot. In this respect, the myth of Orpheus and Eurydice as expounded by Blanchot corresponds completely with the story of Dante and Beatrice – and God: the deeper, more invisible side of the object of desire is invested in the divine abyss that reveals itself in the visible beauty of Beatrice.

10

Beatrice and Eurydice

Blanchot, however, evokes Dante's Beatrice as a counter-image to Eurydice: Beatrice for Blanchot is eminently a vision, whereas Eurydice is essentially *not* to be seen. Kevin Hart, following Blanchot, insists on this contrast, again taking Dante as the model of literature in its most traditional sense and as epitomizing its ideal of vision, its privileging of 'sight':

> Eurydice is the one who resists being seen, who does not come into the light, and in this she is utterly unlike Dante's Beatrice who, as Blanchot says in a late piece, has 'her being wholly in the vision one has of her, a vision that presupposes the full scale of the seeable, from the physical sight that strikes one like lightning to the absolute visibility where she is no longer distinguishable from the Absolute itself: God, and the *theos*, theory, the ultimate of what can be seen.'[1]

Of course, for Dante and for Christian negative theology, God as the Absolute is rather what *cannot* be seen: 'No man hath ever seen God', according to the Gospel of John (1:18), in a passage that echoes a host of other texts in this tradition, including God's refusal to show his face to Moses (Exodus 33:20). And viewed in this light, Beatrice's translucence to the divine turns out to be but a shadow. As a revelation of God, Beatrice is *not* fully seeable. This is so precisely to the degree that she *is* a reflection of the divine. Dante is repeatedly reminded that God essentially transcends his sight, however much the glory of the Divine is refracted in the face – especially the eyes and smile – of Beatrice. The vision of Beatrice is, to this extent, a constant reminder that God cannot himself be seen.[2] Dante's poem ends with the vision of God, but its many metaphors, not to mention its avowals of failure, leave God's essence unseen – or seen as Nothing – even in the final symbolic representations of the mysteries of the Trinity and the Incarnation.

Most important and most precious is precisely what does *not* show up in the face of Beatrice – namely, the divinity that she invisibly mediates. Beatrice is for Dante, finally, a mediation of transcendent divinity, not an end or object in herself. Dante describes her, for example, as 'the one . . . who will be a light between the true and the intellect' (*quella . . . . . che lume fia tra 'l vero e lo 'ntelletto*, *Purgatorio* VI.44–5; see, further, *Paradiso* I.64–6 and XXXI.70–2). In this respect, Blanchot's comparison of her with Eurydice is misleading. This becomes especially clear when Blanchot describes what Eurydice is for Orpheus: 'She is, for him, the extreme of what art can attain, she is, beneath a name that dissimulates her and under a veil that covers her, the deep obscure point towards which art, desire, death, night appear to converge. She is the instant where the essence of night approaches as the *other* night' (*Elle est, pour lui, l'extrême que l'art puisse atteindre, elle est, sous un nom qui la dissimule et sous un voile qui la couvre, le point profondément obscur vers lequel l'art, le désir, la mort, la nuit, semblent tendre. Elle est l'instant où l'essence de la nuit s'approche comme l'autre nuit,* L' espace littéraire, p. 225).

Whereas Beatrice rightly counts as a mediation of divine light from above to Dante, Eurydice is the shadow of darkness that Orpheus would lead up to daylight. Eurydice is a symbol for the ultimate 'object' and goal of Orpheus's vision and passion. Dante's ultimate aim is not Beatrice but rather the luminous and yet impenetrable and vanishing 'point' of the divine.[3] Beatrice is only a mediator. It is with regard to God rather than Beatrice that Dante, in effect, says exactly what Blanchot says about Orpheus's vision of Eurydice: 'Orpheus can do everything, except look this "point" in the face, except look at the center of the night in the night' (p. 225). One must bring this dark side of divine vision, its 'impossibility', into the picture in order to compare Dante's vision with Orpheus's, and then the alleged *contrast* fades in light of how Dante has actually already pre-comprehended the moment of impasse on which Blanchot insists.

Orpheus's desire is to see Eurydice not in the light of day, but in the darkness of the underworld. He wants to see her when she is invisible – and so see the source of his inspiration in the divine night. This is what Dante, too, is persistently attempting – and failing – to achieve in the *Paradiso*. Dante is on a journey to beholding God himself beyond all heavenly appearances, including Beatrice, in whom alone something of divinity becomes visible – while essentially *God* continues to escape visibility. The journey is *a priori* impossible and can be completed only via a miracle.

The attempt – or the temptation – to transgress the divide between the visible and the invisible, or between the creature and the Creator, is what drives the *Paradiso* all along. To seek to know God in himself or in the (for us) infinite abyss of the divine essence – is a transgressive assault upon his inviolable unknowability, as Dante's roster of transgressive humans (and other creatures), reviewed at the outset, clearly registers. It is insinuated already in the original temptation by the serpent in the Garden of Eden: 'ye shall be as gods, knowing good and evil' (Genesis 3:5).

To transgress the separation of God from his creatures by usurping knowledge not commensurate with humanity is the danger that Dante's own masterwork flirts with and worries over and scrupulously claims to avert – over and over again, to its very end. Dante cannot help but see how the quest of his sacred poem is very nearly a repetition of the primeval arch sin of humankind in aspiring to a knowledge making one like God. This is still the issue with Blanchot's Orpheus, even without God, in his coming face to face with night. He is punished for intolerable hubris in seeking and turning to the vision of the Absolute.

Blanchot's reading is, in fact, deeply indebted particularly to Christian elaborations of the Orpheus myth that embroider on the classical sources in terms of both sin and salvation. Interpretations, for example, by Clement of Alexandria and Boethius, connect Eurydice, who dies of a snake bite, with Eve, who is seduced by the snake to commit a mortal sin. Orpheus then becomes a figure for Christ redeeming humanity from the clutches of Hell, and the uncanny power of Orpheus's music naturally interprets the means of this redemption. His poetry is music in which sound and sense are fused in a way that tames beasts, making them understanding and compassionate. This resembles what happens in Dante's *Paradiso*, where language is not exactly divested of its referential, denotative meaning, but rather acquires a higher value, one that cannot be rationally mastered, a surplus of sense that is transmitted directly in the sensuous harmony of the musicality of language.

The tendency to *blame* Orpheus and to emphasize his *failure*, which is characteristic of twentieth-century representations, can be traced to Rilke's 1904 poem 'Orpheus, Eurydike, und Hermes', which certainly influenced Blanchot. Yet the note of failure of the artist or poet in his ultimate task is clearly sounded already by Dante in the *Paradiso* – already from its very beginning, but conclusively and shatteringly at its end, where the highest artistic achievement is finally underwritten by failure. Again we encounter Dante's uncanny capacity to anticipate our own most apparently idiosyncratic sensibilities.

Reading Blanchot's adoption of the Orpheus myth as a symbol for the essential experience of literature back into Dante's quest for divine vision in Paradise in this way restores the characteristic accents of Blanchot's interpretation to their original matrices in Christian interpretations of the myth. Orpheus's descent was taken over from Ovid (*Metamorphoses* X.1–85) and Virgil (*Georgics* IV.453ff) by Church fathers and doctors and projected onto an infinite abyss of divine transcendence (and eternal death and damnation) that was unknown to the classical authors. The Christian moral sense of Orpheus's loss of Eurydice is that we must overcome attachment to worldly loves on pain of death.

The exaltation of failure or in any case the 'apology' for it, together with a certain insistence on its necessity and in a sense superiority, is crucial to Blanchot's approach to literature, and this is what he highlights in his interpretation of the Orpheus myth. Considering the evolution of this myth in tradition, we can see this turn as Christian in its essence and origin. The model of a Christ who saves by the crushing debacle of the Cross marked the myth as it passed from patristic authors like Cyril of Alexandria and Augustine to medieval *Minnesingers*, who celebrated the sacrifice of love also in Orpheus's honour.

Christian self-sacrifice is redemptive and is linked with life-giving creativity especially in Renaissance representations of Orpheus. The lyre is borne as a Cross by Monteverdi's Orpheus, as he freely offers himself to the underworld (*Orfeo favola in musica*, 1607) – thereby Christianizing Polizziano's *Fabula de Orfeo* (1470). Calderòn's *El divin Orfeo* (1636) brings out the world-creating capacity of Orpheus's music, and Gluck's opera *Orphée et Eurydice* (1774) celebrates music itself for its world-renewing wherewithal. The self-reflexive poetic language of the *Paradiso* points already in this direction and also beyond to its deconstruction – lest art become idolatry. However, the myth takes a tragic turn in modern appropriations subsequent to the Christian Romantics, in whom its comic vocation was essentially consummated.[4]

Blanchot's Orpheus loses his (poetic) work for the sake of his *regard*, his direct contemplation of his inspiration. He, of course, also winds up a sacrificial victim himself, torn limb from limb, as punishment. Dante likewise sacrifices himself and his work for the vision of God that infinitely exceeds and renders any human work of his vain. His self-sacrifice for his work registers in the figure of Marsyas in *Paradiso I* and again in the opening verses of *Paradiso* XXV, with their poignant depiction of the poet enduring a lean (*macro*) existence in exile. Most importantly of all, this work itself is sacrificed in the end. Dante's contemplation of the absolute finally bursts his work asunder, and its verses scatter like the leaves of Sibyl.

Yet, in the end, Dante does fix his gaze on the 'point' at the apex of his journey through Paradise, and rather than losing the divine vision he is transfigured beyond himself and beyond time by a superhuman, beatified, divine consciousness. He is transformed beyond mind and memory. What cannot be humanly seized without a grave transgression can nevertheless be graciously granted by a God beyond his grasp, and that is what Dante claims has come about in his experience of the *visio Dei*.

Blanchot, of course, believes in no such possibility. Yet his credo can be critiqued by Dante's as much as the reverse. My contention is that Blanchot is thinking in a space that he has hollowed out of its theological content. That is why Dante's theological poetics help us see what is at stake in what Blanchot is seeing before he banishes or effaces its essential motivations in an effort to purify thought of theology. His refusal, his contestation, his 'transgression' is an inversion of a radical transcendence at the heart of immanence, an irreducible Other, a Stranger, inhabiting our world and us, who was discovered, or invented, most originally in theological terms.[5] Historically, in our culture, such radical transgression of the world and its order of immanence occurred decisively and in a revolutionary new form that continued to ferment throughout the history of the West, resulting in the emergence of the revealed God of monotheism. Blanchot's rejection is perhaps natural and inevitable: it coincides with the general revolt of modernity against its own past as preserved in tradition. Nonetheless, in order to avoid distortion, this revolt must be seen in its infinite indebtedness to what it rejects.

11

Blanchot's Dark Gaze and the Experience of Literature as Transgression

Dante's vision resolving into the god's vision of the shadow of the *Argo*, taken as a symbol for the nature of the paradisiacal vision as a whole, eminently exemplifies Blanchot's theory of literature or poetic vision as consisting essentially in what has been aptly termed a 'dark gaze'. Such is the 'regard' or gaze of Orpheus – a motif that can be traced all through Blanchot's *oeuvre*. There is a moment in Blanchot's first novel, *Thomas l'obscur*, when what the protagonist's eye sees is precisely what prevents it from seeing. Thus: 'Not only did this eye which saw nothing apprehend the cause of its vision. It saw as object that which prevented it from seeing. Its own glance [regard] entered into it in the form of an image at the tragic moment when this glance was considered the death of every image' (*Non seulement cet œil qui ne voyait rien appréhendait la cause de sa vision. Il voyait comme un objet, ce qui faisait qu'il ne voyait pas. En lui son propre regard entrait sous la forme d'une image au moment tragique où ce regard était considéré comme la mort de toute image*).[1]

Kevin Hart refers to this passage in order to explain what he means by the 'dark gaze': 'We have passed from a subject's gaze at an object to an object's gaze at a subject . . .'.[2] Hart continues by quoting Blanchot: 'It is the gaze of fascination in which 'blindness is vision still, vision which is no longer the possibility of seeing, but the impossibility of not seeing, the impossibility that becomes seeing, which perseveres – always and always – in a vision that never comes to an end: a dead gaze, a gaze become the ghost of an eternal vision.'[3]

In this passage, the vision of an object turns into non-objective vision in language. All one can see of being is its shadow because Blanchot's 'vision' is basically linguistic. It therefore operates on a principle of difference without purely, positively visible objects.

Dante's paradisiacal vision is a vision of light and life, of course, yet it is conveyed only in and by shadows. These are, in Blanchot's vocabulary, 'images' that make up the obscurity of the night. What Dante is able to see is only the refraction of divinity in the soul-lights that cover over and dim down the divine radiance. He sees only the darkness that contrasts with the absolute light of divinity. Furthermore, in his attempt to communicate his experience, Dante falls back constantly on declarations rather of his impotence to convey it. He presents reiterated formulations of the ineffability topos rather than the vision as such – to such an extent that this focus on his impasse actually becomes the main content of the vision itself.

Bataille, for whom this passage in Blanchot's novel was a seed of revelation, saw that '"seeing nothing" does not at all announce an ulterior vision but itself constitutes this vision. It is a "tragic" ecstasy because . . . it prepares its own failure. Its "vision" is nothing other than "the death of every image".'[4]

As with the protagonist of *Thomas l'obscur*, Dante's focus, too, is on his own impasse. This is what he 'sees', in his reiterations of the ineffability topos – and what opens into the divine vision. Dante's metaphysics and negative theology are not strangers to this idea in their insistence that what the self sees in its ultimate, divine vision is itself: it sees that it is 'not other' than God, in the terms of Nicholas Cusanus (*De li non aliud*, 1456). The same terms have been used by Christian Moevs to read Dante's experience of God as metaphysical in a non-dualist sense (*The Metaphysics of Dante's Comedy*). Precisely seeing the *impasse* of the self, or seeing the self *as* impasse, is the passage through to the divine vision. Humanity tends to be translucent to divinity in Moevs's non-dualist perspective. However, Dante's insistence on the impasse of ineffability associates him also with an aporetics in which the divine vision comes about in and *as* its own impossibility. This requires something more radical than a negation of negation or a lifting of the barrier. It is rather a dwelling on the barrier – and finding the transcendent precisely there: not in anything that can be represented as above and beyond but rather in the breakdown of reference and the collapsing into the immanence of a self that disintegrates and opens outward into an untamable Outside. Dante theologizes this collapse and breaking open of the self, but he nonetheless passes through mystic death and renunciation of representation and of all his discursive powers. His poeticized theology reads as a metaphor for this experience of non-experience.

There is an urgent question concerning transgression that is posed by this comparison with Blanchot. Does Dante transgress in the sense of opening the whole order of the cosmos to question in his very effort to affirm it? He works radically as a writer pursuing the experience of language to its limits. Does this experience open the field in which Blanchot treads – the 'space of literature' – in which every step is transgressive? There is, for Blanchot, an implosion of all order that is effectuated through writing. And the question is whether or not Dante as a writer participates in this destruction of universal order, in this 'disaster'. Writing entails the implosion of the universe for Blanchot – the 'dés-astre'.[5] This is presumably not what Dante wanted to believe, but it is perhaps inseparable from what he experiences when he follows without reservation the path of writing as his way to God.... Or perhaps Dante's experience can call into question Blanchot's interpretation of the limit experience of writing. For Dante, it is the explosion of our system and the cosmos as we know it, yet he believes that this very explosion opens to God beyond and into a higher order than we can comprehend without divine grace.

12

Negative Theology and the Space of Literature – Order Beyond Order

Poetry can preserve the unknown *as* unknown and thereby *not* efface the neuter. Heraclitus, Hölderlin, Char and Heidegger, in Blanchot's view, do this. And so does Dante, we might now add, in his *Paradiso*. My point is not to say that Dante and Blanchot are saying the same thing or even to claim to bring to light an underlying 'elective affinity'. My purpose, rather, is to use Blanchot to explore the (non)sense of transgression in order to help us understand more completely the meaning that Dante's complex and original form of transgressiveness can assume in our own contemporary critical context.

Blanchot's inclination would presumably be to oppose himself fervently to the religious ideology found in Dante. Dante elaborates a verbal and a symbolic system reiterating the Catholic system of theological dogmas for comprehending all existence and expounding its essence in words. Yet what the *Paradiso* testifies to is the way this system does not exist just for its own sake, but is rather made to serve a movement back into the event or encounter with what no system can explain and what no word can encompass. In the *Paradiso*, theology is ultimately absorbed back into negative theology – into the silence that takes back all that the poem says. This movement undermines the possibility of mastery – of positive dogmatic knowledge of divinity – through forgetting everything in the experience of utter transformation even beyond the human (*trasumanar*) in the encounter with the unknown and unameable.

Dante's words, no less than Blanchot's, are explorations of what escapes words. But Blanchot, like other French thinkers of difference, prefers to restrict this discovery and to attribute it to a canon of modern poets, particularly Mallarmé, Hölderlin, Rilke and Char, and tends to see classical literature and especially Catholic medieval and religious poetry like Dante's as wholly subjected to the model he contests. I counter that Dante also manifests profound sensibility for the neuter that eludes every paradigm, and that he is far from ignorant of what Blanchot calls 'the profoundest question'.

Blanchot demonstrated keen interest in 'Maître Eckhart' from the time of *Faux Pas*, as well as in the mysticism of Nicholas of Cusa and Simone Weil. However, it is hard to to imagine that his response to Dante would not include also contestation and refusal of an apparently assured system of orthodox belief.[1] Near the heart of what Blanchot wishes to refuse is an other-worldly orientation that Dante and the Catholic Middle Ages are so often taken to epitomize. Still, perhaps this outlook should not be conceived of simply in oppositional terms and as an alternative to any this-worldly or earthly orientation.

Blanchot rails against 'the refusal of death, the temptation of the eternal, all that which leads humans to make a space of permanence where the truth can be revived, even if it perishes' (*le refus de la mort, la tentation de l'éternel, tout ce qui conduit les hommes à ménager un espace de permanence où puisse ressusciter la vérité, même si elle périt*, L'entretien infini, p. 46). He is suspicious of all the ways that language can be instrumentalized to establish a secure reign (*règne sûr*). He feels that in bygone times, the gods and God were used in order 'to help us not to belong to the earth, where everything perishes' (*Jadis les dieux, jadis Dieu nous ont aidés à ne pas appartenir à la terre où tout disparaît*, p. 46).

Schematically, Dante would belong on the wrong side of the divide being staked out here. He would stand accused of other-worldly escapism, of fabricating psychological compensations in order to avoid facing death. Yet, more deeply considered, just such schematic rejection is what is being placed into question in the thinking of the neuter. The authentic upshot of attending and adhering to the neuter is *not* the choice of 'this' world in preference to an 'other' world, or of continual change rather than permanence. All such oppositional determinations are released in yielding to the movement of the neuter. And we cannot help but note the contradiction inscribed in the very idea of 'permanent change', since that makes change itself unchanging. Despite his partisanship for the other world and eternal life, Dante makes a movement also of belonging to the earth. It is even his final movement, as he returns from the Empyrean to earth and to the (impossible) task of relating his experience. Beyond being the protagonist of perhaps literature's most famous other-worldly journey, Dante is also the prophet of the *secular* world, for reasons broached by Erich Auerbach and elaborated by hosts of critics in his wake.[2]

Dante's cultural revolution begins with his rendering a vision of 'eternity' dynamic in the historically evolving language of the vernacular. It is in the crease between opposites such as time and eternity, or this world and the other, that Dante opens up a kind of access to the inaccessible – maintaining rather than abrogating, underlining rather than effacing, its inaccessibility, given the fundamentally aporetic nature of his undertaking from beginning to end of the *Paradiso*. Dante's attempt to think and experience eternity in terms of time, and his dwelling constantly close to the impossibility with which he is faced, places him in line with what Blanchot calls thinking the neuter.

Blanchot helps us to understand transgression in terms of the neuter and thus in a sense deeper than that of violating a code of laws – even for the sake of adhering to another code considered as higher. Blanchot thinks of transgression as undoing law and order altogether.[3] He envisages the space of literature as a dimension in which neither the law nor its violation are possible because nothing can be unambiguously defined. Just as Dante presents both a rigid, totalized system and its undoing, so Blanchot's thinking spans this essential tension: 'For if Blanchot is a thinker of extreme possibility, of the literary work as a reaching to the limit, an exhaustion of the possible, of totalization, force, and decision, he is also, simultaneously, and with even greater intensity, the thinker of impossibility, of worklessness, radical weakness, undecidability, and otherness, of writing therefore as an ever futural response to what is unthinkable within the horizon of the present and the same, the familiar, the already known'.[4] As Blanchot himself puts it, thinking moves between 'naming the possible' and 'responding to the impossible' (nommant *le possible*, répondant *à l'impossible*, L'entretien infini, p. 68).

Now Dante presents a cosmos in which all is arranged in a unified, divinely given order. He makes awesomely clear the difference between breakers of divine law and those obedient to and contributing to divine order. Yet he also demonstrates the necessity that any finite formulation of this order finally burst asunder and that all our conceptions of order implode, so as to let the divine have its day and say – the divine that ultimately surpasses all *our* understanding and saying. Dante's vision of universal order at the same time lets us glimpse its limits and even see how it is all poised to come apart – at least when it is put into language. A certain disaster or *dés-astre*, in the etymological sense of undoing or deranging the stars, is discerned by Dante behind his colossal verbal construction. This is for Dante – at the antipodes from Blanchot – the fulfillment of a divine apocalypse, yet his creation and de-creation of the space of literature has far-reaching implications that we can understand better by following how they are worked out in some of their most radical consequences by Blanchot.

Dante criticism has recognized his stance, if not as aporetic, at least as dialectical. Emphasis has been placed, particularly by Giuseppe Mazzotta, on the co-implication of order and transgression. Having asked whether transgression can be absorbed by order or whether, conversely, order is subverted by transgression, Mazzotta concludes that 'order and transgression are not antagonistic terms' and that 'each ceaselessly entails the other in Dante's visionary poetry'.[5]

Following the logic of such a resolution or reconciliation, Mazzotta accurately draws the inference that order requires exclusions: 'Order, it seems, is not the total harmony of existing viewpoints; rather, it is gained at the cost of exclusion of those who transgress the unity of order' (p. 15). This seems to be the only possible response to the questions of violence against transgressors raised by Dante's *oeuvre*. It takes Dante at his word on the problems posed by the tortures of

Hell or by the encomiums for persecution of heretics. However, this result, I submit, points to the inadequacy of staying just at the level of Dante's representations (Dante himself suggests such an inadequacy in *Paradiso* XIX.40–66). Representation indeed requires exclusions. But perfect order is beyond representation: in the end, it can only be God – ineffable, inconceivable simplicity. And it is in this direction that the poem persistently points.

Mazzotta reads the *Commedia* and particularly the *Paradiso* as a poem of force, pivoting on words like *valor* and *virtù* (connoting especially 'power'), which in fact accentuate its opening statements. But we must not ignore the way in which the movement of the poem also works to undo this force and to acknowledge the inevitably negative working of divine power, which can never be simply identified with any force within the world. Mazzota's is indeed a dialectical solution, but there is also a movement altogether beyond dialectics, which Dante performs in jumping out of discourse into silence. Silence is not the dialectical opposite of speech: it opens rather the way to the infinitely or, better, inconceivably transcendent – to the Open and Outside. While Dante believes that he is never essentially outside of God, nevertheless he experiences himself as outside of all possible representation of God and divine order. This is why Dante insists, signally through the ineffability topos, that his poem is aporetic – not just a dialectical synthesis of time and eternity but an encounter with the impasse between them and an experiencing of this aporia to the limit where it turns inside out and takes him beyond himself, beyond subjectivity, in a mystic death that is immersion in God.

Dante's poem undoes what it does – in order that it may be redone from above and beyond his own power. Divine power, too, works in just this way – kenotically, by self-emptying and self-offering. Divine power, in the Christian revelation that inspires Dante, is manifest in the sacrifice of Christ in the shape of a lamb (*Par.* XXIV.1ff) – thus in refusing force and retaliatory violence, all the way to death on the Cross (Philippians 2:8). At the extremes of vision, Dante discovers that the order of God is so sublime that it cannot be understood or interpreted

Negative Theology and the Space of Literature – Order Beyond Order 103

by humans in their language. He is opposite Blanchot in his wish to affirm ultimate cosmic order, yet he still witnesses to the fragility and inadequacy of any order that we can actually grasp and represent in our language. He glimpses the co-implication in disorder of all that can be humanly apprehended as order. This embeddedness of order in disorder is what Blanchot exposes insistently in virtually all his works – sometimes through the motif of the *dés-astre*, literally the 'un-staring' or 'dis-staring', connoting an absence or collapse of cosmos (*kosmos* or 'order' in Greek). Dante's courting this limit of vision accounts for the deep sense of transgression that lurks beneath the surface of his works. Dante's stars become the symbol of a divine order that to humans appears only as chaos. He believes that the universe hangs providentially together, and he is granted vision of this order, yet it turns out to be vision of the invisible and is beyond rational comprehension (*divina providenza, che è sopra ogni ragione, Convivio* IV.iv.11).

Certainly, Dante does not refuse all order. Quite the contrary: His refusals are ordered to an overarching legitimate divine Order for all. Yet this unfathomable Order dramatically exceeds definition and comprehension in human terms – at least as presented finally in the *Paradiso*. The Heaven of Jove in particular emphasizes how all our human ideas of justice are given the lie by the Justice we cannot ordinarily discern, even as it continues to work itself out in our history. Dante's poem is a protest against and a contestation of the world he lives in; it projects another order for the world – one proffered in writing. Perhaps only his *Paradiso* satisfactorily embodies it and does so only by constant declarations of its own inadequacy. As writers like Blanchot have relentlessly emphasized, writing is a gesture of suspension and removal from any actually existing order. Blanchot also stresses how this makes the writer essentially an exile, an errant wanderer. The writer is outside every articulable order. Writerly creation occurs as essentially prior to every created order.

Dante's journey may at first seem in every way to be the opposite of errant wandering. He knows where he is going! And he maps out with precision at every level – from the moral and symbolic to the sensorial and topographic – exactly where he is at every step along the way. And yet this assiduous charting can flip over into its opposite in the *Paradiso*, where he dwells on the fact that the goal and organizing principle of all is the great Unknown! That realization relativizes everything that Dante supposedly 'knows'. It is all as nothing in relation to the final goal that orients his journey and the universe – and *that* remains *un*known to him in his radical inadequacy or 'disagguaglianza' (XV.83). There are many ways and means of mediation, of course – an entire universe of analogy. Yet Dante ever again confronts the uselessness of all his artificial measures vis-à-vis the experience of Paradise and its measureless first principle ('God'). He is, then, the poet whose condition is necessarily one essentially of exile, as in Blanchot's description: 'He leaves, he becomes the one whom Hölderlin calls the wanderer, the one who, like the priests of Dionysius, wanders from country to country in the sacred night' (*Il part, il devient, comme l'appelle Hölderlin, le migrateur, celui qui, comme les prêtres de Dionysos, erre de pays en pays dans la nuit sacrée*, L'entretien infini, p. 323).

Part Two

Authority and Powerlessness (Kenosis)

13

Necessary Transgression – Human versus Transcendent Authority

What, then, does this consideration of transgression inherent in language and literary experience, such as Dante and Blanchot discover it, have to do with transgression in the more familiar social and political senses of the word? 'Transgression', in its primary acceptation, is a moral and legal concept. We know that Dante did not theorize about language in the abstract. He envisioned it concretely in its socio-historical contexts embroiled in the power struggles that were tearing his world apart.

The social and political implications of Dante's thought about the (dis)order of the world have concerned, among others, Giuseppe Mazzotta, who describes in terms of 'transgression' the manner in which Dante transcends ethics into a sphere of love and freedom beyond the reach of law: for Dante, as for Augustine, 'the foundation of the world lies in love and freedom. Love refuses commandments and is at one with freedom. Appropriately, Dante's *Paradiso* contains no ethics, in the conviction that ethics would be incongruous in the divine economy'. Consequently, one of the two key problems or hermeneutical challenges facing Dante scholars is 'establishing how Dante's fiction of order adapts the forms of transgression'.[1]

Mazzotta specifies this inherently transgressive sphere beyond ethics as one of ludic play and aesthetic performance in the *Paradiso*.[2] Accordingly, the *Commedia* maps Dante's progression from 'an ethics of laws and prohibitions', in *Inferno* and *Purgatorio*, to the ludic displays and spectacular performances of *Paradiso*, which subsumes ethics in the interplay of the good and the beautiful in art.[3] There is no possibility of moral error (or equivalently, we might say that in perfect freedom and spontaneity there is only errancy, *errare*), so Paradise is all cosmic song and dance. The poem comes undone in a sense not of loss, but of gaining 'heaven' beyond restrictive rules of language and history. Such an incalculable yet inescapable divine economy resembles what Bataille (in *La part maudite*) and those following him, like Derrida, call a 'general economy' that regulates covertly any 'restricted economy' defined by oppositions.

Dante poetically uses the language particularly of theology in order to transgress human authorities of all types. Attuned to this aspect of Dante's vision, Mazzotta envisages transgression as implicated in order and as instrumental to lending life and dynamism to Dante's vision. Mazzotta brings out how the language of theology is inherently transgressive of logic.[4] Dante follows Boethius and Anselm in highlighting the paradoxes of the Incarnation that force him into transgressions of logic such as the oxymorons of the Prayer to the Virgin in the last canto (XXXIII.1–39). Language about God is inherently transgressive, since, as Anselm suggested, the divine Word is above and beyond grammar: perhaps all words are improper as used of God.

Another eminent example, Alain de Lille's *Rythmus de Incarnatione et de septem Artibus* (*Patrologia Latina* 210), displays the breakdown of grammar specifically vis-à-vis the Incarnation: *In hac verbi copula / Stupet omnis regula* ('In this copula of the Word / Every rule is stupefied'). The divine Word in its infinite creative freedom contains a contradiction to every finite word bound by the rules of grammar, as Alain's verse pithily states. Extrapolating from grammar to the arts and sciences, Mazzotta maintains that 'Dante draws a picture whereby the pattern of theological order is a transgression of the order of the sciences: the Virgin is a mother and a daughter of her own son: the circle of the geometers cannot be squared. This meant that the discourse of theology is itself a supreme transgression of the rules of grammar'. Incarnational theology, 'in which the poem is rooted and from which it takes its energy', is all a transgression of the rationality of the sciences known to man in his finitude (Mazzotta, 'Order and Transgression', p. 18).

The theology of the Incarnation, of a transcendent God immanent in human form, fully God and fully man, baffles logic. For it declares infinite divinity to be paradoxically present in its plenitude in the finite form of an individual human being. This bursts the categories of classical, Aristotelian logic and leads to a dialectical logic for mediating contradictions. Hegel, largely inspired by the revolution of thought inherent in Christianity, rethought logic along dialectical lines. Of course, Hegel's systematization would be vehemently contested and rejected in postmodern times. Nevertheless, all the attacks by poststructuralist French thinkers are still deeply beholden to Hegel, whom they struggle against and yet fail to surpass, as is acknowledged by Derrida in *Glas* and elsewhere. Dante likewise, I submit, remains unsurpassed, as much as our age wishes to think itself done with the other-worldliness for which Dante's 'divine vision' stands as an icon. Depending on how we interpret it, Dante's poem embodies transgression in as radical a sense as we can imagine.

Dante's utopian political vision, with his appeal to a transcendent authority, inevitably positions him in the ambiguity between being an arch-transgressor and an arch-accuser of transgressors. He must transgress against human authorities in order to obey the transcendent authority of God. This is not just a choice to accept one authority rather than another ranged on the same plane of possibilities. Dante aligns himself on a vertical rather than a horizontal axis: he perceives and acknowledges true authority of an absolutely exceptional sort, one from which all order in heaven and on earth devolves. In obeying this divine power and its dispensation for the world, he is also positioning himself to oppose all exercise of authority that runs counter to it. This he indeed did with tenacity, becoming thereby the sworn enemy of the chief powers of his day – particularly the papacy, the French crown and the government of Florence. As much as he longs for a concrete institutional incarnation of divine authority, in his embrace of unconditional freedom and love he inevitably transgresses any merely human instantiation of it: his prophetic radicalism commits him to 'transgression' of any codified laws and ethics. Yet, any human individual inevitably proves to be imperfect as an impersonation of power.

14

Dante and the Popes

Dante lashes out savagely against ecclesiastical authorities all through his poem. In *Inferno* (VII.46-8), coming upon the avaricious in the fifth circle of Hell, he does not shrink from pointing out specifically the clergy, who are made conspicuous by their tonsures. Numerous popes and cardinals (*papi e cardinali*) are included here as especially culpable of this vice. From the first canto, Dante targets even the highest ecclesiastical authority, with the allegory of the she-wolf (*lupa*) hungry for territory (*peltro*) and mating with other animals. This figure for a greedy papacy metamorphoses later – in the closing visions of *Purgatorio* – into the image of the whore of Babylon fornicating with the kings of the earth (*Purg.* XXXII.148-53). Dante borrows the latter image from the *Apocalypse of St. John the Divine* and uses it to prophetically figure the depravity of the popes.[1]

Among the most pungent of Dante's portraits of sin and among the most audacious of his crusades as a writer is the attack he mounts against papal corruption embodied in the person of Boniface VIII (Benedetto Caitani), together with his predecessor Nicholas III (Giovanni Gaetano Orsini) and their successors in simony, Clement V and John XXII. Yet, even as Dante vigorously denounces the leaders of the Church from the top down, he also takes pains to demonstrate his respect for and submission to ecclesiastical authority in general and in particular to the office of the papacy. He fulminates against individual popes, whom he feels have betrayed their sacred trust, consigning a series of them to a most opprobrious damnation in the holes of the third *bolgia* in the eighth circle of the Inferno (canto XIX) and delivering them up finally to the passionate denunciation of St Peter's diatribe in *Paradiso* XXVII.19-26. Still, Dante's transgression or revolt is never against papal authority per se but always only against certain egregious *abusers* of that authority.

The very canto of condemnation for the *individuals* who had worn the 'great mantle' (*Inf.* XIX.69; cf. 'papale ammanto' in *Inf.* II.27) most recently at the time when Dante writes testifies to his 'reverence for the highest keys' (*la reverenza de le somme chiavi*, *Inf.* XIX.101) of Saint Peter. He thereby endorses the power invested in the clergy to unlock or block the gates of heaven. Indeed in *Purgatorio* XIX.127-39 Dante kneels down in reverence before a penitent soul upon learning that he had briefly filled the office of the supreme pontiff as Hadrian V. In the next canto, through Hugh Capet's sordid vision of his successors on the French throne, Dante even sides with the pope's offended dignity: Hugh condemns the outrage committed against Boniface VIII in 1303 at Anagni by Philip IV (Philippe le Bel), King of France, through his representative William of Nogaret in collusion with Ciarra Colonna, member a Roman family inimical to Boniface (*Purg.* XX.85-90). Dante goes so far as to compare the wronged pope taken captive to Christ suffering at the hands of Pilate, since the pope, for all his personal perfidy, nevertheless remains the 'vicar' of Christ on earth (*nel vicario suo Cristo esser catto*) and the head of his body, the Church.

It is clear, then, that Dante does not understand his attacks against the popes as transgressions against papal authority as such, which he fully respects, if it is correctly defined and rightly deployed. His attacks are rather attempts to redress transgressions on the part of individual popes against the divine disposition of things. Such overstepping of the bounds of papal authority began, Dante believes, with the Donation of Constantine. According to the legend that Dante follows (*Inf.* XIX.115-17), the Emperor erroneously rewarded pope Sylvester with a secular realm in exchange for having healed him of leprosy. He had no right to do so, and the consequences for history, as Dante sees them, were calamitous, notwithstanding Constantine's good intentions, for which he is blessed in the heaven of the just. The ever-growing pretensions to worldly power on the part of the popes culminated in Dante's own time in Boniface's arrogant absolutism. Boniface expressly declared in his bull *Unam Sanctam* (1302) that the pope has the right to depose emperors and to judge all authorities whatsoever on earth, while being himself subject to none.

Opposing such unwarranted papal interference in the temporal sphere, Dante understands himself to be fighting against the real transgressors. He must violate the unjust decrees of men in order to remain faithful to the providential plan of God. He acts on the strength of his prophetic authority, which trumps the authority of priests, even the highest priests. He wields this prophetic authority by the direct inspiration of a divine revelation that imposes on him a duty to correct and castigate the erroneous exercise of power within human institutions, beginning with the Church and its priesthood.

The crucial distinction between transgressing against God's authority and revolting against human authorities who themselves betray it is developed by Dante in filigree in relation to a minor figure from biblical narrative named Uzzah. According to 2 Samuel 6:2-7, God struck Uzzah dead because he touched the sacred Ark as it was being brought back to Jerusalem after being recaptured by King David in war with the Philistines. Only Levites had the right to handle the Ark and other sacred things. The punishment seems severe and is intimidating, since Uzzah was only trying to steady the Ark when 'the oxen shook it' and placed it in danger of falling. Dante cites Uzzah as an example serving to warn those who would presume to usurp priestly offices that have not been officially conferred on them (*per che si teme officio non commesso*, *Purg.*, X.57). He accords zero tolerance to such usurpers of an authority not their own as granted by God.

In his epistle to the Italian cardinals, Dante imagines that his adversaries might taint him with the fault of Uzzah for meddling as a layman in ecclesiastical politics. Uzzah is punished evidently for unauthorized encroachment on priestly prerogatives, and thus *prima facie* he is a warning to someone like Dante. Dante retorts, however, that he is not touching the *Ark* but only the stumbling oxen that put it at risk of falling (*ille ad arcam, ego ad boves calcitrantes*, *Epistle* XI.12). He does so as the least among believers, one with no pastoral authority whatsoever and yet one, like the prophets, consumed with zeal for the house of the Lord (*zelus domus eius comedit me*, XI.9). Thus, he acknowledges that there are special powers reserved for the clergy, yet the men who assume them are not beyond critique as to whether they exercise such authority properly. The crucial distinction is that Dante is not interfering with things of God and the legitimate exercise of priestly functions, but only endeavouring to correct those human beings who are failing in their responsibilities to fulfil truly divine duties. Dante's apparent nearness to an exemplary transgressor is thereby turned around to serve in an accusation lodged by him against the *real* transgressors, whom he fiercely denounces with his own special brand of holy indignation. In effect, he lays claim to a prophetic authority outranking the power of the priests.

15

Against the Emperor?

Just as Dante upholds the principle that one man, the Pope, should exercise undivided spiritual authority on earth, so he subscribes to the principle that incontestable command over human wills in the temporal sphere should belong to one man, the Emperor. Here again Dante finds fault with specific individuals and their exercise of this office, yet he adheres to the ideal of a despotic power cast in the image of the one God supreme over all. He aims to reproduce the indivisible authority of God in heaven by its embodiment in a single human individual on earth. This formula, however, seems to be a prescription for inevitable transgression on the earthly plane, for the individuals in whom such power is vested are imperfect. The perfect Empire Dante yearns for resembles the 'illustrious vernacular' (*vulgare illustre*) in being an ideal that cannot be realized concretely and historically. Dante hunts in vain for the perfect language, which is like a panther leaving its scent everywhere, yet being apprehended in no language actually spoken anywhere in Italy (*pantheram . . . redolentem ubique et necubi apparentem, De vulgari eloquentia* I.xvi.1).

Emperor Frederick II, the *stupor mundi*, was the last Holy Roman Emperor to effectively exert imperial sway in Dante's historical era. Yet Frederick was a condemned heretic, and Dante does not flinch from recalling this (*Inf.* X.119). Furthermore, Dante rejects Frederick's view of nobility as consisting in inherited wealth and refined manners (*antica ricchezza e belli costumi, Convivio* IV.iii.6). Dante was anything but obsequiously submissive to the authority of this individual, whom he nevertheless admires, especially in *De vulgari eloquentia*, as an enlightened monarch who created a court in which poets flourished.[1] The emperor and his son Manfred are glorified as 'illustres heroes' pursuing humanistic ideals and spreading nobility and rectitude (*nobilitatem ac rectitudinem sue forme pandentes*, I.xii.4).

Dante, in fact, goes to great lengths in *Convivio* IV.viii–ix to defend himself against inferences that by taking a position against the imperial opinion (*l'opinione imperiale*), he might be irreverent (*inreverente*) towards the Emperor or in contumacy (*tracotanza*) of imperial authority. He explains that the Emperor has unlimited power to command human action, that his office extends to mastering human will like a chevalier (*cavalcatore de la umana volontade*, IV.ix.10), but that the definition of nobility (*gentilezza*), like that of youth (*giovinezza*), is not a matter that can be determined by human will. These questions are determined by the nature of the things themselves, and therefore the Emperor's opinion in such cases is not binding. In other words: Give unto Caesar what is Caesar's and unto God what is God's, writes Dante (IV.ix.15), echoing Matthew 22:21.

As with the individual popes condemned for simony, so the individual person of the Emperor Frederick II remains condemned for heresy as he appears in Dante's *Inferno*. Consequently, the absolute authority Dante exalts in both the secular and the spiritual spheres remains intact, but of the order of an ideal. The office is respected, but not the individual man who fills it, at least not if he deviates from the right path and true. Transgression of humanly prescribed limits, against laws set up by men, even those in the highest positions of authority, is authorized for Dante by appeal directly to God. His prophetic self-confidence in the end will not cringe before any humanly institutionalized forms of authority, whether priestly or imperial.

16

Inevitable Transgression along a Horizontal Axis

Despite the daring and audacity of his polemics against individuals, Dante in his self-assured aplomb seems, then, after all, to deserve his standing as authoritative poetic voice of Roman Catholic theological orthodoxy. He challenges certain dubious, popularly held beliefs (like the assumption of St John's physical body into heaven) and controversial doctrines (like those concerning the time before the angels' fall and their possession of memory), yet he shows no sign of doubt that this religion is the sole authentic repository of divinely revealed truth and the unique way to salvation for all humankind. In the eighth heaven of the *Paradiso*, in order to prove himself impeccable in the one true faith, like a well-prepared undergraduate or 'bachelor' (*come il baccialier*) triumphantly passing his exams, Dante unhesitatingly rattles off to Saint Peter in person the official credo of the Roman Catholic Church – albeit fused with Aristotelian metaphysics of the Unmoved Mover (*Par.* XXIV.130–47). Of course, especially given this last 'scholastic' metaphor, the whole scene might be heard as echoing with an ironic ring.

Still, at least at first, it does not seem right to attribute to Dante a will to transgress the recognized authorities of his life and times. He contrived excruciating punishments for all conceivable forms of disobedience. He does not wish for a world in which authority can be lightly traduced and law be violated with impunity. Nevertheless, there are aspects of his vision and vital *élan* leading him ineluctably into transgression. In order to obey his sense of a divine summons to a prophetic calling, inevitably he runs into conflict with the authorities and institutions that reign in a corrupt world. Limits set even by apparently legitimate authorities on earth are inevitably transgressed in his effort to steer his course by the vertical lodestar that guides him – the higher authority of the divine.

Ulysses in his 'mad course' goes to his damnation along a horizontal trajectory across the ocean that ignores the God above until it is too late, and his ship sinks down 'as pleased an Other' (*come altrui piacque*). His transgression is, in the first place, a blindness to this verticality – whereas Dante is guided by it all along the way. Dante's trespassings on the horizontal plane against earthly authorities are relativized and righted by this vertical axis. They take on thereby a sense completely lacking from Ulysses's merely horizontal displacements and over-steppings. Indeed, the Ulysses canto is set in a prophetic framework through a contrastive allusion to the figure of Elijah, whose chariot is seen to be drawn straight up to the heavens by its horses (*vide 'l carro d'Elia al dipartire,/ quando i cavalli al cielo erti levorsi*, XXVI. 35–6). This vision is accorded Elisha, Elijah's disciple and successor as prophet in another kind of vertical descent down the genealogical tree. Dante, like Ulysses, accepts no limits set by authority on the horizontal axis: he too voyages metaphorically beyond the Pillars of Hercules, especially in his journey through the heavens. Yet he, in contrast to Ulysses, heeds a calling from on high and ultimately from above all finite determinations.

Defiance of God's rules and restrictions is nowhere condoned in the *Commedia*. However, the interpretation of God's will and ordinance for mankind is a matter that Dante does not allow any human magisterium to determine definitively, at least not without being accountable to God and thus also to those who can truly interpret God's will. His theory accords a human ruler despotic powers, but he also shows himself willing to transgress any worldly power in the name of the higher and indeed absolute power of God.

We have observed that Dante is remarkably harsh in his attitude towards transgressors. Although he was himself censured (or would be) as a transgressor by the authorities of both Church and State, most severely by the government of his own country, the Florentine Republic, he himself sides passionately and unequivocally with the principle of institutional power wielded with full force to stomp out opposition.

Paradiso XII's encomium of the divine 'athlete' and combatant who descends like a raging torrent upon heretical outgrowths gives unqualified approval to the violence of Saint Dominic in rooting out heterodoxy. And Dante sets no limits of law to what methods the Emperor might employ to destroy those who resist his rule. Dante's model of authority is absolute despotism.

Paradoxically, however, Dante takes this attitude precisely from the position of a transgressor and a flagrant one at that, a thorn in the side of the authorities reigning in his day. And this is not just an accident. He *must* transgress these earthly, accommodated and compromised systems of authority in order to assert the absolute, divine right that he believes should reign on earth as it does in heaven. In his own understanding and intention, he is not only *not* a transgressor but is called to be an uncompromising critic and relentless castigator of all who transgress the divine ordinance for the world. Nonetheless, in the perspective of the governments of men, Dante was a transgressor and lived in exile and even under condemnation to death.

17

Heterodox Dante and Christianity

Numerous readings of Dante would identify him completely with the heroic, martyred transgressor of otherwise unchecked church tyranny.[1] Some portray him as a free and fiercely secular spirit who is refractory to all dogma, a philosopher persecuted on account of the danger he represented for the Church and its oppressive power. Others range him among the spiritual Franciscans or in a tradition of transgressors that can be traced from the Cathars and Waldensians. This heterodox Dante is the arch-rebel persecuted by the Church, as well as by his own city of Florence, for having courageously served divine justice by his unyielding denunciation of the misdeeds of the high and mighty. This Dante is a martyr for human freedom.

Many interesting questions arise here about the nature and degree of Dante's transgressiveness especially of the ecclesiastical authorities of his day and particularly of those at the head of the institution to which Dante himself publicly pledged allegiance. In a slew of esoteric interpretations, Dante is portrayed as the arch-antagonist of the central teachings of the Church – especially those concerning the afterlife and salvation in Christ alone through adherence to the Catholic faith. This critical tradition is the one most intent on envisioning Dante as deeply and deliberately a transgressor, particularly in the spiritual and intellectual orders. I wish to read with and against this critical tradition in order to isolate what is accurate and compelling in such approaches from what entails ideological programmes motivated by extraneous interests.

Such interpretations often portray Dante as a radically heterodox author who only pretended to be a champion of orthodoxy in order to elude persecution by the Inquisition. According to this reading, the real meaning of his poem would have been kept a secret: its esoteric message would be expressed in a code intelligible only to the initiated.[2] Obvious allegories such as the *Veltro* and the DXV, which call for decoding yet resist adequate explanation by the usual interpretative means, serve as points of departure for systematic reinterpretations of the poem in thoroughgoing esoteric terms, typically as secretly transgressive of the orthodox faith with which it overtly aligns itself throughout.

This esoteric, hermetic Dante is most often made out, as by Robert Bonnell, to have been the champion of a philosophical doctrine for initiates who rebelled against Catholic orthodoxy.[3] Adriano Lanza offers a sober and sophisticated interpretation of Dante as drawing from Gnostic, currents, especially in the neo-Manichean form given to them by the Cathars.[4] However, the point of all religious commitments in this outlook is to transcend sectarianism towards world unity in the perspective that all religions are one. Gregory Stone argues that Dante abhorred institutional Christianity and was inspired by a vision of a post-Christian philosophical unity of all humankind in which no particular religion would have any privilege.[5] Medieval Islamic humanist philosophers following Al-Farabi and up to Averroes and Ibn Arabi had developed the kind of vision that Dante pursues by adapting their ideas and disguising them at the same time, so as to evade inevitable chastisements.

According to numerous versions of this revisionary interpretation, Dante would have expressed himself as a believer only in order to avoid the otherwise sure condemnation and destruction that awaited him at the hands of the Inquisition. Readings such as Stone's maintain that Christianity 'is not his real creed, which is instead the creed of the philosophers'. For Stone, Dante professes the Catholic *Credo* 'only as a ruse by which to fool an inquisitorial Church of Rome' (p. 277).

The idea that Dante did not say what he meant out of fear of being persecuted by the powerful and particularly by ecclesiastical powers consorts ill with the fact that Dante did express himself in the most inflammatory terms against precisely these authorities. What he published in his poems and letters is saturated with provocation of virtually all the effective institutional powers to which his world was subject, most especially the clergy and popes. So why interpret his embrace of faith as only a pretense in order to hide an underlying defiance of religion and its priests that he dared not avow? He included in his poem even express injunctions to say it all and let the powerful scratch where it itches (*Par.* XVII.112–29). It does not seem at all like Dante to pull punches. Surely, he believes what he says in his profession of faith, in his religious fervour that goes beyond philosophy, and in his denunciation of the specifically identifiable men he feels are betraying the divine offices of Christ. However, a narrowly bigoted rather than a truly 'catholic' vision of faith could hardly have satisfied Dante.

Dante's characteristic gesture is not so much a deliberate choice to be a transgressor as an embrace of principles in all their radicality, an embrace which reaches so deep as to upset certain narrowly orthodox interpretations of them. Dante transgresses fundamentally in a horizontal direction against human powers not by a will to resist authority in the human sphere per se but through his adherence to a transcendent divinity imposed as if vertically from above. Stone presents Dante as not really a believer in divine transcendence but rather in the truth of human reason or philosophy. Christianity, with its focus on a transcendent life and other-worldlinesss, is for Stone what Dante is intent on overcoming through turning away from the Augustinian Middle Ages and opening towards the European Renaissance. I believe, rather, that for Dante in his finally desperate utopianism, human reason itself at its limits breaks open to a theological transcendence that drives him ineluctably to transgression of any actual human social and political rule.[6]

What *is* profoundly accurate about Stone's view is that Dante is not satisfied with only other-worldly recompenses but is intent on realizing justice *in this world*. Thus, effective authority is imperative for him here on earth. He wishes to realize a truly just government that would tolerate no transgression. Dante is anything but the confirmed outlaw who finds that being a transgressor, after all, suits his rebellious temperament. On the contrary, his works cry out for one law for all, for one universal State. His marginal status as exile is dolorously tolerated as a bitter necessity for an interim period that he wishes with all his heart to end as soon as possible.

Yet, by intransigent adherence to a transcendent order and authority that he is not content to let be *only* for another world, Dante is compelled to transgress all human obstacles that stand in his way – or rather in *its* way. The very tenacity of his obedience to this transcendent vision turns, paradoxically, into his cantankerousness vis-à-vis all this-worldly authorities. Surely this expresses his personality, but it is also written into the Christian Testament – notwithstanding all its injunctions to meekness. Christians are not predisposed *a priori* towards being transgressive. Rather the opposite is the case. And yet in the world such as it is and always has been, transgression for them is nevertheless inevitable, as is exemplified anew by the testament of Dante's life and writings.

18

Christianity: An Inherently Transgressive Religion?

The reading of Dante as an independent, free philosophical thinker becomes implausible when it ignores the fact that Dante declares himself, without reservation, to be committed to exercising the severest authority against all transgressors of God's will and the institutions that represent it. Dante is not just an innocent victim of persecution against transgressors; he is himself zealously concerned with expunging transgression. He is, therefore, not just by accident or mistake in conflict with the authorities of his time; his mission compels him to challenge and to mortify those authorities. We can surmise, moreover, that from a prophetic perspective such as his, virtually all eras and their institutions would stand in need of such denunciation.

Saint Paul did not want to stir up trouble with the authorities ('Let every person be subject to the governing authorities', Romans 13:1) because no conflicts were worthwhile except spiritual ones: 'For we wrestle not against flesh and blood, but against principalities, against powers, against the rulers of darkness of this world, against spiritual wickedness in high places' (Ephesians 6:12). Yet, even in his case, the inevitable conflict with earthly authority in the name of the heavenly is patent, and he eventually died as a martyr for it. As soon as Christians understand themselves to be called to fight for justice on earth, they are bound to transgress against authorities that they deem to be not in accord with Christian ethics or, more profoundly, with divine love.

Dante attempts to realize a divine command or transcendent order in the immanence of the historical world. He does so poetically, since politically he was stripped of power with his expulsion from Florence after a brief term as member of the city's governing body, the

Signoria. His Christian religion itself is based on such a paradox from its inception. Jesus of Nazareth for Christians is God Incarnate – the transcendent God immanent as a fully human presence on earth. We should remember that Christ himself became a transgressor and was killed as such – as an outlaw nailed to a cross between two common criminals likewise crucified. The New Testament frequently recalls that the Scriptures (especially Isaiah 53) had indeed prophesied that the Messiah would be punished for our transgressions and be executed as a transgressor. Dante is prone to transgression of human order in obedience to a higher command that nevertheless lays claim to being honoured as divine revelation even in the immanence of the human. It comes to him through prophetic revelation. There are thus much deeper theological reasons for Dante's adherence to Christianity than just the coercion of power, as in Stone's hypothesis.

Christianity itself, deeply understood, is radically transgressive.[1] Dante understands it so. He glorifies Saint Francis's rebellion against his earthly father and his inherited social class (*Par.* XI.58–9). In spite of his ideal of a universal Church and Empire, in practice Dante must be a transgressor against human authorities. What human being who actually assumed it could possibly fulfil the office of supreme spiritual or temporal authority in a way that Dante would not have to condemn and correct, as he does with the popes and emperors? True authority for Dante is God's and no man's – except to the extent that a human being exercises power completely in accordance with God's will.

What is, nonetheless, so provocative about Dante's perspective is that he does expect the transcendent authority he obeys to be incarnated immanently in the State, as well as in the Church and its clergy. This repeats the paradox on which Christianity is founded. It creates (almost) ever-lasting tension between what *must* be and what *is*: one must constantly protest and, yes, transgress against the laws that are laid down by humans – for the sake of respecting the true law of God. This tension is what makes Dante seem to swing vertiginously between two radically different versions of Christianity: the glorious Church Triumphant of Rome, with all its mighty power and hierarchy, and the original, apostolic church founded in a kenotic spirit of poverty. The former is pragmatically necessary to discipline an immature and wayward human race, but the latter is the more authentic image of spiritual liberty. Dante's impossible ideal embraces elements from both of these divergent models.[2]

In its more deeply reflective and speculative variants, Christianity acknowledges its inspiration by an ideal beyond formulation: transcendent divinity potentially enjoins to transgression of every formulated law. The invisible Source is always more than and beyond any visible form, and faithfulness to the divine Person can entail transgression of any positive precept. Even the interdiction against murder can be relativized, as in the story recounting Abraham's willingness to sacrifice his own son (Genesis 22). Infinite freedom, such as Christianity proclaims, is incompatible with unconditional allegiance to any externally given law. Paul's antinomianism in Galatians and Romans expresses this spirit of inevitable, even if reluctant, transgressiveness.[3] And Jesus himself transgresses the laws of the Sabbath, since '[t]he Sabbath was made for man, not man for the Sabbath' (Mark 2:27). He is ready to transgress all laws that do not serve the human freedom to love.

Whether Dante deliberately intended to assume the role of a transgressor and aimed to propound radically subversive ideas are questions of a psychological order and not perhaps soluble. More important than inferences concerning Dante's personal preferences and convictions is the issue of what his works and their afterlife reveal about the nature of transgression and its place in human history and society. Does Dante perhaps contribute to revealing Christianity to be an essentially transgressive religion? The novelty of Christianity in Western culture flows from the idea of a transcendent God that nevertheless becomes incarnate in history and even issues normative directives to humans. Although this God is infinite and humanly ungraspable in his own being or essence, nevertheless he claims to become present as an individual man and to act in the finite sphere of human relations. He even issues concrete, determinate judgements – or at least specific invitations and appeals to do justice – in the words of the Gospel.

This is a paradox: the wholly transcendent has become utterly immanent. Jesus makes divine transcendence humanly immanent: he is God in his humanity at its most vulnerable, without exclusion even of death and despair. But Dante sees at least a practical moral necessity for this impossible state of affairs. His reasoning, worked out most consequentially in *De monarchia*, is that absolute power can create absolute peace and all the benefits of society that flow from it. If humans accord unconditional authority to one finite individual, this individual's authority is unconditional and as good as infinite. This individual can operate practically as the Almighty: disinterestedly, and so as perfectly just. This is Dante's answer to the question of how to define and deal with transgression. If it is a secular solution, it is still based on the monotheistic model of one transcendent source for all authority.

Dante reveals the predicament that transgression cannot be confined to the margins of the social order and history as one of the momentous results of Christianity's transcendent and yet immanent God. In Dante's vision, the existing social and historical order must rather be upset by a transcendent order that is prophetically apprehended and announced. And yet Dante, especially in *Monarchia*, claims to discern this order concretely as rationally necessary rather than only as revealed: or rather, the revealed in this case is nothing but the absolutely and purely rational. Dante is the prophet of a secular society. This is crucial to the argument of Stone's book, as it builds on Auerbach's work and the tradition of a secular Dante.

I believe, however, that it is wrong to portray Dante as this-worldly *rather than* other-worldly, as on the side of reason more than of revelation, of philosophy more than of theology, of the secular and universal more than of his Christian faith. Dante aims rather at the fulfillment of these opposed terms each in and through the other. He would renounce neither the rational universality of his vision nor the singularity of his Christian faith in its claim to be the unique revelation of the fullness of truth. Stone is often polemical in advocating the secular over the religious. His purpose is to redress what he perceives as an imbalance in the critical reception of Dante and in the pervasive Christian bias of

Western culture. In the end, however, Stone, too, is generally prepared to embrace the coincidence of opposites, following philosopher-theologians in the tradition of Meister Eckhart and Giordano Bruno and Nicolas Cusanus. They all thought *ratio* or *intellectus* through to the point where it bursts all boundaries and opens into the infinity of divinity. This line of thinking is kindred in spirit with Dante's project: he does not discard reason but expands it by the poetic word, opening it to infinity and thereby ultimately to 'God'.[4]

Stone's book raises the provocative question of whether Dante is not inevitably in the position of a transgressor, or rather of whether his thinking is not inevitably suspected of transgressing – precisely in its claim to universality and authoritativeness. Dante does make a claim for the authority of philosophy, but reason remains inseparable from transcendent and theological authority. He also makes a claim for the absolute truth of Christianity, and yet he exposes its hypocricies and validates pagan and Jewish traditions as prefiguring a truth that finally transcends all figures whatsoever.

Dante's exaltation of human reason and philosophy does not take them as known quantities in human or worldly terms, as if philosophy could suffice. Like Meister Eckhart, he exalts intellect in its capacity of self-transcendence and of (dis)identification – or of unselfing – in the divine. Reason for him is that part of the human soul that is divine (*preziosissima parte de l'anima che è deitade*, *Convivio* III.ii.19). Dante's humanism should not be taken in the sense of a reduction to the human or to 'this' world. It is finally a *transhumanization* (*Par.* I.70) that opens towards the other world, the divine world – or the world as *un*known and *un*defined.

If there is scant philological foundation for the esoteric readings of Dante in the name of specific brotherhoods or heretical groups, apart from the general impregnation of the philosophical culture of the time with hermetic traditions, the astonishing mushrooming of esoteric readings today is itself highly indicative. Dante opens history and tradition, with their pretended intimations of eternity, to interminable interpretation. The nature of his text is to place the weight of transcendence upon particulars which take on a symbolic significance that cannot be contained. His texts (like the most original poetic texts in all times) shatter finite codes and yet invite appropriation by every imaginable attempt to interpret the unconditionally true. So every creed can make its attempt to appropriate him for its particular concerns.

Following Christ, Dante insists on an immanent realization of transcendence. For Christ, however, this cannot take the form of an exertion of power or authority. It is rather through the critique and reversal of all earthly power that the advent of the divine takes place. Dante realizes this deconstructive truth of Christianity in his exploration of language and his reaching the limits of language in the *Paradiso*. Politically he appears to believe that there is one right form of government. However, this remains but an ideal – in his time and in any time. Any actual imperial power exercised by fallible humans is bound to become subject to subversive and scathing attack such as Dante levels unsparingly.

Transcendence is realized in the world through the infinite critique and deconstruction of worldly powers. This is a vital truth of the Christian religion as rediscovered particularly in our time.[5] It is communicated in very powerful and decisive ways by Dante's poetry, even though certain of his prejudices and ideological commitments as an individual appear to be *prima facie* contrary to this negative theological perspective. Beyond his personal opinions and passions, Dante's role in the unfolding of the Christian vision consists essentially in his pursuing the possibilities of poetry to express all reality – and the divine 'Nothing' from which it all derives – to the limit of the inexpressible. This is the bearing of his final work, the *Paradiso*, in all its elusiveness.

Of course, it would be erroneous to assume that Dante held only one consistent position throughout his career. He is obviously committed to authoritarian social models, and yet an independent, critical consciousness is unmistakably in emergence in his works as well. The *tension* between divergent perspectives is what is made manifest in his poetry. The propulsion towards heterodox beliefs is disclosed as erupting from within orthodox convictions themselves. This is what brings Dante close to 'transgression' of paradigms in the radical, deconstructive sense. Rather than being rejected and so remaining intact as violated norms, the paradigms transgress themselves: they open to a space of ineffable otherness surrounding them.

The absolutely immanent realization of absolute transcendence is the paradox that is in play with Dante's language that deconstructs the sign in order to become direct manifestation of divinity as a differential play of signifiers and significances (as in *Paradiso* XVIII, discussed in Chapter 2). The infinite authority that Dante reverences can actually be manifest only in the dismantling or deconstructing of all finite claims to authority.

Placed within this paradisiacal problematic, even Dante's embrace of the absolute power of Rome turns it inside out: it becomes absolute powerlessness. That alone, as in the Cross of Christ, makes manifest truly transcendent, monotheistic power, which levels and obliterates all merely worldly power – power existing unto itself.[6] The esoteric meaning of the *Commedia* is, in this sense, one of unlimited transgressiveness *and powerlessness.*

There is, accordingly, an aspect of the typical esoteric reading of Dante that stands at the antipodes with respect to the interpretation I am advocating. Esoteric readings often aim to reveal the one true meaning of Dante's text by decoding its secret language. But this model of a 'closed semiotic system' is just what the inherent transgressiveness of Dante's signs makes impossible. Their meaning cannot be confined to any system: it is achieved precisely in springing them all open. This way of understanding Dante's text extends far beyond the common esoteric approach for which '[t]he prophecies are interpreted within a closed semiotic system made of signs, of numerical indices, of structural equivalences . . .' (*Le profezie vengono interpretate all'interno di un sistema semiotico chiuso, fatto di segni, di indizi numerici, di equivalenze strutturali . . .*).[7] This way of understanding Dante makes him a sectarian and entails an *un*Christ-like assertion of power. The deeper inspiration of the heretical approaches themselves is, in fact, exactly the opposite. The point is to open access to a common, humanly universal truth rather than to become an adherent of an exclusive mystery society. Such universality is generally affirmed by adroit esoteric readings, at least when they refrain from attempting to fit Dante to the procrustean bed of a single secret code to which they alone hold the key.

Part Three

Transgression and Transcendence

Everything about Dante's life and testament points in the direction of a preoccupation with the issue of transgression: his passionate concern with fostering a universal and inviolable world order; his obsession with vengeance and punishment of transgressors; his having been condemned by his own city to death by burning, should he be found trespassing upon the territory of the Florentine Republic. Add to this his self-assertion as an original author, in some respects perhaps the first self-consciously modern author and in any case one that defies the limits of the human in his journey of self-fashioning by poetry, which becomes a means of 'transhumanization'. Seen from these multiple angles, Dante's life, thought and writing all revolve around the issue of transgression and the great problem of how to deal with it justly and efficaciously.

What is transgression for Dante? In modern poetry since Rimbaud, if George Steiner is correct, there is an 'epistemic break' around 1870: from this moment, poetry begins to work against language, against *logos*, and to become transgressive of reason and its rule, to work against the grain of language in its natural expression of the real.[1] This notion of transgression of reason and its *logos* has been further enriched in the twentieth century by the Freudian discovery of the unconscious. Words are undermined by unconscious intentions expressing themselves in slips or shifts that subvert their consciously willed and rationally intended meaning. Against reason and its control erupts another message, another meaning: the voice of the Other. Can the seed of this historical transmutation be found already harbouring in the seams of Dante's medieval masterpiece?

Dante's transgressiveness is not so much against reason, certainly not against reason per se. He still strives after a transcendent reason that exceeds and countermands finite human reason, which is itself but a part of divinity. In *Convivio* III, Dante explains how Love, as first cause, 'reasons in his mind' (*Amor che ne la mente mi ragiona*). As has already been noted, reason is itself the part of the mind or soul which is divine (*quella fine e preziosissima parte de l'anima che è deitade*, III. ii.19). It is, in effect, the *Verbum* that is in infinite excess of all human reasons. In the *Paradiso*, Dante imagines that this mystery of the Word comprises an 'occult' side of the universe.

> *'Colui che volse il sesto*
> *a lo stremo del mondo, e dentro ad esso*
> *distinse tanto occulto e manifesto,*
> *non poté suo valor si fare impresso*
> *in tutto l'universo, che 'l suo verbo*
> *non rimanesse in infinito eccesso'.*
> (*Par.* XIX.40–5)
>
> 'He who turned his compass
> at the limit of the world, and within it
> distinguished so much that is hidden and manifest,
> could not impress his worth on the whole
> universe in any way that did not leave
> his Word still in infinite excess'.

This divine Word (*Verbum, Logos*) is at the same time the source of human rationality and cannot be fathomed without the exercise of human reason. Therefore, too simple an opposition is misleading. Of course, Dante's own statements do often employ an oppositional logic. Yet Dante's transgressiveness is not against the divinely ordained order of things: on the contrary, he is the uncompromising champion of the absolute and ideal order that supersedes and contradicts the actual perverted and abject state of fallen humanity.

Most importantly, beyond all Dante's ideological declarations and his claims on behalf of a transcendent divine authority, his poem enacts transgression of an altogether different sort, one that does not know how to say even what it transgresses, one that transgresses *itself* and transgresses everything it could possibly stand on in order to make its own claim. This is the transgressiveness that bears some resemblance to what Bataille and Blanchot explore under the rubrics of 'inner experience' or 'contestation', as well as 'transgression'. In it, not just defiance of some specific authority is at issue. Rather, a seed of impossibility within any positive attempt to establish order (a 'restricted economy', in Bataille's language) is discerned.

19

Transgression and the Sacred in Bataille and Foucault

Blanchot's essential insight concerning transgression and the sacred is formulated in terms clearly indebted to negative theology by Michel Foucault in an essay interpreting the work of Georges Bataille. Foucault's 'Preface to Transgression' aims to explain why this term 'transgression' has become particularly indispensable in our time. The reason is that in contemporary culture there is no longer any *positive* notion of the sacred. The sacred today can be approached only indirectly through its opposite, through a profanation which transgresses it. Such transgression is a 'scintillating', or perhaps rather a sentient or 'knowing' ('scientillante') form of absence of the sacred:

> Now a profanation in a world that no longer recognizes any positive meaning in the sacred – is this not more or less what one could call transgression? In the space that our culture gives to our gestures and our language, transgression prescribes the only way not to find the sacred in its immediate content but rather to reconstruct it in its empty form, in its absence rendered thereby sentient.
>
> *Or une profanation dans un monde qui ne reconnaît plus de sens positif au sacré, – n'est-ce pas à peu près cela qu'on pourrait appeler la transgression? Celle-ci, dans l'espace que notre culture donne à nos gestes et à notre langage, prescrit non pas la seule manière de trouver le sacré dans son contenu immédiat, mais de le recomposer dans sa forme vide, dans son absence rendue par là-même scientillante* [sic].[1]

In a modern world in which the sacred no longer has any positive meaning, transgression emerges as the only way of recovering a sense of the sacred – even if only as absent or missing. This makes profanation intrinsic to the manifestation of the sacred – as in the parodic and often perverse sacramentalism of *Finnegans Wake*. It also acknowledges theological revelation as essentially negative in character. Like the God of negative theology, the sacred is known primarily through what it is *not* and therefore as absence or 'empty form'. In this manner, transgression itself becomes the essential nature of the event signifying the divine.

Dante does not ignore profanation as an aspect of the total revelation of the divine in his 'Comedy'. Especially the *Inferno* attests to how profanation and sacrilege are crucial to the manifestation of the divine in human life as perverted in a fallen world.[2] Dante is thus no stranger to the sense of transgression that Foucault articulates. The difference is that the emptiness of which Foucault writes is for Dante an emptiness relative to us and our human language, which can express nothing of God's own proper nature. But what to us is emptiness is actually, in God's own reality – or at least so Dante imagines – a higher plenitude than we can grasp.

The logic of transgression as a revelation of limits and an evocation of what lies beyond them, as expounded by Foucault, is perfectly applicable also to Dante's project and its final *oltraggio* ('beyondness', from 'oltre' – 'beyond', XXXIII.57). 'Transgression is a gesture that concerns the limit' (*La transgression est un geste qui concerne la limite*, p. 754). Only this limit manifests it in 'its totality' (*sa totalité*). Furthermore, 'The limit and transgression owe themselves to one another' (*La limite et la transgression se doivent l'une à l'autre*, p. 755). The point where the limit is passed is 'the glorification of what it excludes; the limit opens violently on the unlimited and finds itself carried suddenly away by the content it rejects; it is realized by this alien plenitude that invades it all the way to the core' (*glorification de ce qu'il exclut; la limite ouvre violemment sur l'illimité, se trouve emportée soudain par le contenu qu'elle rejette, et accomplie par cette plénitude étrangère qui l'envahit jusqu'au cœur*, p. 755).

Foucault develops these reflections in transparently negative theological or apophatic terms. He recognizes transgression as bringing interior illumination, as marking the space of inner experience with its sovereignty before 'growing silent, having given a name to the obscure' (*se tait enfin ayant donné un nom à l'obscur*, p. 756). Transgression opens a space beyond ethics and its oppositions. It is *not* negative. It 'affirms limited being and affirms it in terms of the unlimited in which it surges up, opening it for the first time to existence' (*affirme l'être limité, elle affirme cet illimité dans lequel elle bondit en l'ouvrant pour la première fois à l'existence*, p. 756).

This affirmation, which is transgression, is a quintessentially apophatic affirmation: with no positive content, it is intransitive affirmation of nothing but itself, since nothing can limit it (*cette affirmation n'a rien de positif: nul contenu ne peut la lier, puisque, par définition, aucune limite ne peut la retenir*, p. 756). As pure transgression, as pure difference, it is a 'non-positive affirmation' (*affirmation non positive*, p. 756), and Foucault recognizes that this is what Blanchot called 'contestation' (*Cette philosophie de l'affirmation non positive, c'est-à-dire de l'épreuve de la limite, c'est elle, je crois, que Blanchot a définie par le principe de contestation*, p. 756). Foucault describes 'contestation', in terms that could serve as well for apophatic mysticism, as going to the heart of the void or 'the empty heart where being attains its limit' (*contester c'est aller jusqu'au coeur vide où l'être atteint sa limite et où la limite définit l'être*, p. 756).

In asking why there is no discursive language for this experience, Foucault modulates from Blanchot to Bataille, the author of *Inner Experience*. Contrasting him with Sade as author of a language of desire, Foucault remarks, 'The language of Bataille on the other hand collapses without ceasing in the heart of its own proper space, leaving the insistent and visible subject naked in the inertia of ecstasy ... extenuated on the sand of what it no longer can say' (*Le langage de Bataille en revanche s'effondre sans cesse au coeur de son propre espace, laissant à nu, dans l'inertie de l'extase, le sujet insistant et visible ... exténué sur le sable de ce qu'il ne peut plus dire*, p. 759). The transgressor lacks a language, and the experience of transgression needs rather 'to speak in the very hollow of the failure of its language' (*parler au creux même de la défaillance de son langage*, p. 759).

Bataille's eye turned upwards and turned against itself (*l'oeil révulsé*), towards the bone, becomes a figure for inner experience and transgression: it does not signify anything but rather marks its own limit. It is self-reflexive, turned back on itself, yet sees nothing in the hollow of the skull and is plunged into the abyss of night. For Foucault, this indicates 'the moment when language, having arrived at its confines, erupts outside itself' (*Il indique le moment où le langage arrivé à ses confins fait irruption hors de lui-même*, p. 765). Foucault finds here, just as we find in Dante's *Paradiso*, 'the return of language upon itself in the moment of its collapse' (*le retour sur lui-même du langage dans le moment de sa défaillance*, p. 766) – in order to open into and towards the Unlimited.

20

Transgression as the Path to God – the Authority of Inner Experience

We saw that even while Dante defies the popes, he nonetheless genuflects reverentially to the institution of the papacy. He clearly intends to respect – and insists that others likewise respect – hierarchy as essential to the universal providential order established by God to keep humankind on the straight and narrow path to salvation and the good life. And yet humanly instituted hierarchy is no longer valid in the next life. Pope Hadrian V bids Dante to rise from his knees immediately, since the former pope is now just a fellow servant ('conserve', *Purg.* XIX.134) of Christ. In the afterlife, we are all equal as siblings and free of all invidious hierarchical subordination.

Already on the Mountain of Purgatory, above the line where atmospheric perturbations cease because all is perfectly conformed to divine order (as Statius explains in *Purgatorio* XXI.38–73), it is no longer necessary to exercise forceful authority. Coercive hierarchical command is suspended and transcended. Before entering into the Earthly Paradise at Purgatory's summit, Dante is *crowned* and *mitered* – metaphorically made king and bishop of his own will (XXVII.142). He is now free to roam at pleasure in the Garden: restored to its original perfection, his will is free to please God by naturally delighting in all good things *ad libitum*.

Authority and hierarchy are necessary for peaceful co-existence on earth, and yet human and institutional hierarchies no longer apply in the afterlife. Worldly institutions with their power structures may be a perverted image of heavenly authority – something like the way Dante's vision of the celestial hierarchy in the Primo Mobile inverts the actual sequence of the nine angelic orders in the Empyrean, since the largest and most outward circles are closer to God, who, however, in the visible model is represented as the central point of light and therefore as closest to the smaller, inner circles (*Par.* XXVIII.46–87). Heavenly authority may be without hierarchy and rather like the circle whose centre is everywhere, while its circumference is nowhere. This is the nature of God, according to the Neoplatonic sources that Dante uses, such as *De causis* and the *Book of the Twenty-Four Philosophers*, and ultimately all authority is God's alone and indeed God himself: hierarchy is consummated in God – in oneness without limit.

Our perspective on transgression may change radically and 'transgression' become in crucial ways the opposite of what it was, when we cross the threshold into the realm of the divine nature. Stepping beyond – literally *trans gredior* – may become the step that enters into the plenitude of actual experience of the divine rather than the step that violates divinely decreed law enforced by other-worldly sanctions. Transgressing, as stepping beyond, at this point is actually keeping in step with the unlimited freedom of the divine. In this sublime sphere, all that happens takes place in a holy transgressiveness. Transgression, as a stepping beyond, is finally the path to God.

Surely, Dante does not abandon all authority in his ultimate vision, but where is this authority now located? In some sense, it has to be everywhere, in every individual, in every reader addressed. This is the side of Dante that has made him a prophet of the modern world and likewise made him a hero in all ages for 'spirituals' of every ilk longing for revolution and emancipation for all. Smuggling counter-authoritarian ideas into the theological arena, the 'French connection', in the likes of Blanchot and Bataille, as well as of Foucault and Levinas, still works to the rallying cry that 'inner experience' is the only true authority. Dante believes in a higher, a divine authority, and yet the point of access to it is likewise through his own conviction and the irreducibly individual experience that he dedicates his life's work to relating. He is in this regard aligned with myriad modern prophets, not excluding eventually Luther, who will make inner experience in some form the highest court of appeal for conscience.

Like Bataille and Blanchot, Dante, too, in effect absolutizes 'inner experience' – which, as for them, opens to an outside.[1] That is why he is able, for example, to say, concerning the number of wings of the seraphim, that Saint John is *with him* (*Giovanni è meco, Purg.* XXIX.105) and in contradiction with Ezekiel. He rather astonishingly takes his own experience in Paradise as authoritative basis for adjudicating this contradiction in the letter of Scripture.[2] Dante delivers an original, authoritative version of Christian doctrine based on his own direct visionary experience of the mysteries of Paradise and the afterlife. This interiorization of truth and doctrine is, of course, deeply Christian in tenor and inspiration.

Christianity is a religion that interiorizes truth, emblematically in Christ's Sermon on the Mount (Matthew 5–7), where the commandments are made to concern not outward acts but an intention or disposition of heart. The authority of 'inner experience' in Christianity at its origin and in its radical renditions is not without pertinence to Bataille's understanding of transgression and Blanchot's sense of contestation. In *Inner Experience*, Bataille actually credits Blanchot with the seminal insight that inner experience is its own authority. He describes a 'new theology' as emerging from his reading of and even personal conversation with Blanchot. Bataille quotes a key description in Blanchot's *Thomas l'obscur* – the one discussed above in the section on 'Non-Vision' – as the germ of inner experience, and then comments:

> Outside the notes of this volume, I know only of *Thomas l'obscur*, where the questions concerning the new theology (which has only the unknown for its object) are pressing, even though they remain hidden there. In a way completely independent of his book, orally, and yet in a manner lacking nothing of the sentiment of discretion which demands that in his presence I thirst for silence, I heard the author establish the foundation of all 'spiritual' life, which can only:
> - have its beginning and its end in the absence of salvation, in the renunciation of all hope.
> - affirm of interior experience that it is the authority (but all authority expiates itself),
> - be contestation of itself and non-knowledge.

Transgression as the Path to God – the Authority of Inner Experience

En dehors des notes de ce volume, je ne connais que Thomas l'obscur, où soient instantes, encore qu'elles y demeurent cachées, les questions de la nouvelle théologie (qui n'a que l'inconnu pour objet). D'une façon tout indépendante de son livre, oralement, de sorte cependant qu'en rien il n'ait manqué au sentiment de discrétion qui veut qu'auprès de lui j'ai soif de silence, j'ai entendu l'auteur poser le fondement de toute vie 'spirituelle', qui ne peut:
- *qu'avoir son principe et sa fin dans l'absence de salut, dans la renonciation à tout espoir,*
- *qu'affirmer de l'expérience intérieure qu'elle est l'autorité (mais toute autorité s'expie),*
- *qu'être contestation d'elle-même et non-savoir.*[3]

Like Dante and other writers in the tradition of negative theology, Blanchot and Bataille pursue inner experience to the limit of the Unknown. Blanchot discovered this experience eminently in Meister Eckhart.[4] It entails a mystic death of the self, in the tradition that Eckhart did so much to foster.[5] Kevin Hart, in the first chapter, 'Art or the Mystical', of his book on Blanchot, traces within the work of Blanchot and Bataille these references and a dense web of reflections touching also on Cusanus and Teresa of Avila and John of the Cross. All tend to show that the quest for 'inner experience' is transgressive because all known norms and principles are necessarily violated. Blanchot also calls this the 'essential solitude' of the artist and the work, since it cannot be supported or authenticated by any standards or criteria outside itself.

Blanchot frequently stresses that literature must be self-transformative and transgressive of religious codes and dogmas – a contestation of authority. Hart observes that 'the art and mysticism of value to him contest their authority without end' (p. 36). Even more than Bataille, Blanchot is centrally interested in the relation of inner experience to literature, and he does not see this experience as incompatible with poetry. Writing entails self-transformation and sacrifice – 'a ceaseless questioning that undoes its own claims to authority and indeed to power' (ibid.). This quest is pursued under the aegis of 'inner experience' by Bataille and Blanchot, with different nuances in their conceptions of how such 'experience' relates to art and to mysticism.

Dante's art and mysticism likewise are emphatically experiential. He filters all the doctrine and culture conveyed in his poem through personal experience re-presented as the experience of his protagonist. Even his 'metaphysics' are experiential, as Christian Moevs has shown in detail, and as such they are 'transgressive' in the sense of inner experience developed by Bataille and Blanchot: his experience, taken as revelation, disrupts and reorganizes all 'known' doctrine. Transcendence becomes transgression in Dante in a way provocatively analogous to what happens in the writings of the modern French writers. Indeed the 'transgressive' aspects of literature and specifically of writing explored by Blanchot are realized spectacularly by Dante in the *Paradiso*.

Both Bataille and Blanchot insist on the primacy of experience, and Dante, too, centres his whole vision on a first-hand experience capable of revising all dogmatic knowledge of theology and cosmology alike. This first-person witness is rendered explicit by forms of the verb *vedere*, *vidi*, etc. *Vidi* ('I saw') occurs 46 times in the *Paradiso*, starting from the fifth verse. Of course, the experience is of the *limit* of experience and even tips or precipitates into what is best described rather as non-experience.

Bataille and Blanchot focus on experience especially as experience of the Unknown. Dante's writing what is impossible, so far as representation is concerned, and as if under erasure, in the shadow of the ineffable God, brings him into the proximity of these French writers. As Blanchot explains in 'L'expérience-limite' (1962), experience is enabled by non-experience. Both Bataille and Blanchot seek the 'experience of non-experience', as Blanchot phrases it. Hart distinguishes their respective emphases in this common quest as follows: 'where Bataille sought raptures occasioned by meditation, Blanchot opened himself to nonexperience by writing: the sacrifice of words and the author' (p. 47). Such experience of the limit and of the sacrifice of himself and of all his words in an approach to the absolutely transcendent is constantly evoked likewise by Dante as the final limit of his vision and as what originates and in the end obliterates all that he writes.

In the opening lines of the *Paradiso*, Dante writes that in approaching its ultimate desire the mind deepens so much (*si profonda tanto*) that memory – which as Aristotle points out in his *Metaphysics* is necessary to experience – cannot follow it. Yet Dante understands the experience in question as the vision of God: he is compelled to present this overwhelming experience of non-experience as homage to the divinity. At the same time, his non-experience entails a transgression of all common knowledge – of all that can be said – concerning this deity. To understand Dante's impasse in its character as transgression, we can be helped by the experiences and reflections especially of those two unsparingly radical theorists of transgression and contestation who were Maurice Blanchot and Georges Bataille.

Experience runs up against the threshold of non-experience also in the tradition of Christian mysticism, from which Dante's discourse is inextricable. Christian renunciation and the *via negativa* are in the spirit of this acknowledgement of a non-experience at the core of experience. This is what Dante truly cannot name. He uses the vocabulary of Christian theism, but he is also quite clear that any vocabulary whatsoever is inadequate to his experience in his ultimate ascent, which is not even properly 'experience' in the end: experience, too, is realized only as negated.

Speaking out of a German mystic tradition that stretches from Eckhart to Cusanus and Silesius Angelus and strongly impresses French philosophers like Derrida, Achim Wurm stresses that 'no experience' or non-experience is at the base of mystical speech: 'In so far as mystical speech is not adequate to mystical experience, it does not originate from such experience either but originates out of Nothing, since it is based on no experience' (*Insofern die mystische Rede der mystischen Erfahrung nicht entspricht, entspringt sie ihr auch nicht, entspringt sie aus dem Nichts, denn keine Erfahrung liegt ihr zugrunde*).[6] This is what makes mystical speech so uncannily free. Dante's discourse in the *Paradiso* is an actualization of the freedom of language that realizes its own utter freedom in unlimited transgression – stepping beyond all limits so as to unite mystically with the Unlimited.

Blanchot and Bataille, as thinkers of transgression, take Christian theology and mysticism as their starting point. To project Dante forward to their thought on transgression in some sense completes the circle and restores the matrix from which they have theorized transgression. By their means, we have endeavoured to elucidate transgression for our own time in the light of Dante's greatly ambiguous and admittedly contradictory – yet not incoherent – transgressiveness. This exposes a sense in which the sacred can be found only kenotically by a complete emptying of all that we hold to be sacred, in order that only the wholly Other and Impossible – and not our idols – fill this space of the sacred.

21

Transcendence and the Sense of Transgression

Dante transgresses the laws of men in the name of the transcendent authority of God, yet ultimately he transcends authority and law altogether: he envisages their grounding in what is beyond law and order and beyond any graspable concept, including 'transcendence' itself. It is a movement (like Creation) of openness and giving ('dante', in Italian, from *dare*, to give) outward. This does not invalidate the theological metaphors he uses: it rather validates them precisely *as metaphors* for what can have no proper language. He thereby undermines all pretensions to a straightforwardly literal truth that would remain within the order of representation. Dante's poem in the end projects itself outside any regime of representation.

Dante is willing to transgress every authority standing in his way, but always in a spirit of upholding the divine authority to whom humans are freely bound.[1] All are without excuse, moreover, should they transgress this one ultimate authority. But can it, then, be represented in the categories of law and order? Dante's higher or transcendent authority is indeed intended to be embodied in institutional and human form. Yet this embodiment turns out to be infinitely open and porous because it has to be critiqued from infinitely far above any actual human realizations of it. Although he is advocating the rule of institutions that exist concretely in the Church and Empire of his time, Dante is utopian in demanding that they possess a purity beyond their real capacity. Demanding concrete institutional realization for the impossible ideal of divine justice, he remains perpetually in eschatological tension.

As on the moral plane so also at a semiological level, Dante's appeal to transcendence turns out to be an appeal to absolute immanence.

This is the way language works in Dante's taking it to its limits in the *Paradiso*, where it has no object to refer to and so presents transcendence immanently in itself and as freed of all external restrictions. Self-reference and free self-expression are its intrinsic structure and nature. But this 'self' is, of course, one that un-binds and is un-bound. It has no internal structure that it does not give up in opening entirely to the Outside. That is the perfection of its own nature, and in this it is God-like.

For esoteric readers especially, this opening is the very realization of the divine in the human. Theological orthodoxy still resists compromising the divine transcendence: strictly positive or kataphatic theology thinks that it needs to have clearly intelligible representations of this divine transcendence. Of course, by necessarily excluding immanence, such representations actually compromise the true transcendence without limit or exclusion that Dante's poetic language enables and requires us to fathom and divine.

In the language of the *Paradiso*, all finite limits are suspended in a collapse of all externally imposed order. There is no longer any representable order of things surrounding or subtending human history, which opens apparently into pure contingency. This would bring about sheer chaos except that the order is all there already as intrinsic to the self, every self, and as unbounded by external limits. This would be perfect order, indeed it is an order like God's – so perfect as to have no form or definition. This is the true nature of order in its source and origin – the divine simplicity itself. It is an ultra- or supra-order that does not exclude transgression, but rather coincides with it. The theological transcendence Dante envisages is ultimately beyond every definable order – it necessarily transgresses all such order. This transcendence, moreover, inhabits him and potentially every individual who surrenders to the vision of God.

Within the terms of his poem, Dante is not finally a transgressor. He crosses every threshold, but unlike Ulysses he is invited and summoned to do so by the supreme deity and author of the universe. Of course, this is initially just Dante's own imagining; it is sure to be true only within his work. The work could all be a solipsistic fantasy, but Dante certainly does not want to settle for that. This is why it is important to see how the work is turned towards its own outside – towards 'God'. Transgression is transgression of itself, stepping across all boundaries and barriers, even those erected or simply imposed inevitably by itself. This absolute relation to the Outside is more determining for Dante's work than any of its own qualities or shaping forms and structures. All the work's own principles and rules are in fact transgressed in the course of moving towards the absolutely Unfathomable. The work disposes of itself as a self-consuming artefact in order to open upon this Beyond.

Dante sees himself as unlike Ulysses, as not transgressive, because of his vertical relation to a transcendent divinity, yet he is willing to transgress every actual authority on earth in his pursuit of this transcendent calling, such as it is created and imagined in his work. This entails transgression, finally, even of his own work for what is beyond it – like the inner experience of contestation taken up by Bataille and Blanchot. Dante creates and destroys his own work in order to open to the experience of the Outside. His transgression of every known authority or law or limit is for the sake of the Unknown.

In opening to the Outside, to the absolute authority of the God it does not know or comprehend, Dante's work transgresses against all known and worldly authorities. It must, in the end, transgress against itself as well. It subverts its own language. In this sense, transgression is its final testament and not only a phase that is subsumed and brought into line with familiar orthodoxy in the end. The sense of transgression in the *Commedia* would be ultimately to transgress all order – especially the intricate order it creates by its own masterful artistry, with all its finely drawn distinctions and its nuanced succession of thresholds – in order to open upon the unknown Outside transcending all order as we know it. This gesture contains the core of what is enucleated through notions such as 'sovereignty' by Bataille. It is thought through by Blanchot in his own peculiar web of notions, including precisely the Outside (*le Dehors*).

In '*Parler, ce n'est pas voir*', Blanchot imagines a turning from human history towards 'the absence of the work'. Every important literary work at its centre flips over into an *un*working. This produces an 'absence of the work', which is 'the other name for madness' (*le désœuvrement: l'absence d'œuvre. – L'absence d'œuvre qui est l'autre nom de la folie,* p. 45). Dante needs the 'mad flight' of Ulysses in order to realize his work as an unworking that opens to the Outside. Dante evacuates his work, in the end, in order to go beyond it towards what is no work of human hands – nor of signs either, although precisely the transgression of signs, and therewith of all humanly defined and mediated order, takes him there.

What Dante discovers – an insight that Bataille and Blanchot will rediscover and rework – is that the final step/not beyond that completes his journey and brings him to God is as much a gesture of deconstruction as of creation: it is achieved by the sacrifice of his own work, by unworking and by the absence of the work, in which the work that he has elaborated and the order of the cosmos it embodies and imitates is transgressed and discarded. This entails 'sovereignty' in the peculiar sense of the radical French authors, and it is sublime.[2] Dante's poem finally exceeds the beautiful that it has so prodigiously created in a movement that shatters its own construction. The poem's triumphant beauties are but blasted fragments left in its wake.

Dante is, in fact, still dangerously like Ulysses – in spite of the mythical structures he has erected to differentiate his own mission from this predecessor's insane escapade. Hence the spectre of Ulysses continues to haunt him all the way to the end of the poem. This is explicitly attested by Dante's last backward glance at the earth. Just before his own crossing to the limit of the physical universe in the ninth heaven, looking beyond Gades at his world's Western boundary, he alludes to 'the mad passage of Ulysses' (*il varco/folle d'Ulisse, Par.* XXVII.82-3). The imagery of 'flight' and 'wings', used all the way to the very last approach to God (XXXIII.139; cf. XXV.50) and noted earlier with regard to Icarus and Phaethon, also subtly recalls Ulysses's 'making wings of his oars' for his 'mad flight' (*de' remi facemmo ali al folle volo, Inf.* XXVI.125).

Dante is especially like Ulysses, moreover, when we consider his transgression semiotically. In the plot of his poem, he accords himself divine authorization, but in his experiments with language in the *Paradiso*, he ventures out beyond all human limits in a 'transhumanization' that surpasses all barriers, all 'signs', in some sense transgressing even beyond signification itself. He is 'divinized', to employ the vocabulary cultivated originally in Alexandrian theological tradition from Clement and Origen to Athanasius and Cyril – except that his step beyond is also a step *not* beyond the human. It is rather a transformation that falls back within the human, even while breaking the human open to what is outside and beyond it – a *trasumanar* that knows no limits and opens into the Unknown, which is taken by Dante to be the mystery of God.

The human in Dante, as also in postmodern culture, discovers in itself a dimension of transcendence that cannot be comprehended within any worldly terms. By virtue of this dimension, the human is itself a 'transhumanization'. It discovers the transcendent at work in the immanent, the divine incarnate in the human. This is consonant with Christian revelation and is, in essential ways, inspired by it. There is also a very postmodern twist to this movement of transhumanization that could be traced from Nietzsche's conception of the *Übermensch* – the 'beyond-human' personified. My point is that this transcendence is discovered as piercing the sphere of immanence and the human individual itself at dead centre. Dante discovers this and enacts it in his poetry at a narrative level in the drama of descent through Hell to the centre of death, followed by resurrection to life in Purgatory, and finally by elevation to eternity in Paradise. He discovers it simultaneously at a semiological level through the deconstruction of the sign – or through the implosion of language that has lost its external object. Consigned to forgetting in the end, Dante's vision opens to the undivided, 'terribly ancient' dimension that is erased by the articulations of memory and culture. All this is a rediscovery of the immanence of transcendence in the wake of Christ. This is what modern culture has largely lost and yet is still searching for. In writing the *Paradiso*, Dante breaks a path that reflection on writing has continued to follow down to its contemporary exponents, including eminently Maurice Blanchot.

This quest has been pursued by Dante and postmoderns alike. It has been pursued more confessedly under the sign of transgression by postmoderns and yet was clearly marked as such already by Dante. What is transgression for Dante? For the mature Dante of the *Paradiso*, transgression is the transcending of all linguistically imposed limits and legalities towards what is called infinite freedom and love in the vocabulary of Christianity – notably the esoteric Christianity of heterodox readings of Dante. These readings emphasize Dante's humanism and the immanence of the divine to the spiritual faculties of humans. Dante is certainly influenced by this type of humanism in its myriad medieval manifestations, but he turns this human awakening back towards its source in 'divine' transcendence. And yet the sense of this transcendence is not to be found except by transgressing all its possible formulations.

The sense of transgression in Dante's *Paradiso* is ultimately one of *non*-transgression, of being outside legality altogether and in the region of the ineffable, where it is no longer possible to transgress because all limits and definitions have been suspended. This experience of transcendence is the basis for the setting down of limits that so preoccupies Dante in his poetic representations. This is transgression in a sense that, in its relevance to our world today, can be productively approached and illuminated through the thought of 'contestation' in the vein of Blanchot and company. This thinking is very far removed from the ways Dante himself would have conceived of transgression, but it develops directly from the work of poetic language in its approach to the ineffable set in motion by Dante's poem and pursued particularly in modern poetry down to our own time so obsessed with what it cannot say.[3]

Appendix*: Levinasian Transcendence and the Ethical Vision of the *Paradiso*

> The negativity of the *In* of the Infinite – otherwise than being, divine comedy – hollows out a desire that cannot be filled and that feeds on its own growth and exalts itself as Desire – which moves away from satisfaction – in the measure in which it approaches the Desirable.
>
> (Emmanuel Levinas, from 'Divine comédie', in *De Dieu qui vient à l'idée*)[1]

Prolegomenon concerning the scope of ethics

Ethics is *prima facie* concerned with what one does or should do. Philosophically, it belongs to an arena distinct from fundamental inquiries into *what is* (ontology) and into *how we know* (epistemology). Yet, at certain junctures in intellectual history, ethics becomes more than that. It becomes essential to interpreting all realms of philosophy and of life. Ethics comes to be understood as fundamental to any disclosure of the world and to the very consciousness of self. From this perspective, what things are and how we know them cannot even be considered until an ethical relation has been taken up vis-à-vis others and perhaps even vis-à-vis an absolute or divine Other. Cosmology, or the representation of the universe, and epistemology, or the foundations of knowing, become irreducibly ethical matters and must necessarily be grasped in ethical terms. Ethics in this sense is more than one branch of knowledge among others: it enfolds in embryo a comprehensive vision of the world and its conditions of possibility.[2]

What does it mean to have an ethical vision of human existence and relatedness in the world? How does life look when viewed through radically ethical optics? Certain intellectual projects push the ethical point of view to its limits and reveal its scarcely fathomable depths of significance. Among them are those of Dante and Levinas. The famous Dantesque, or possibly pseudo-Dantesque, 'Letter to Can Grande' classifies the *Paradiso* as ethical or moral philosophy (*morale negotium, sive ethica*, Epistolae XIII.16.40). This may strike us as somewhat surprising, given the sweeping cosmological and metaphysical scope of the poem. The encyclopedic embrace of all knowledge and culture, natural and divine, makes the poem philosophical in the broadest and highest sense. But evidently all this philosophy and general knowledge is to be understood as in essence ethical. According to this outlook, it is as ethics that the significance of any kind of knowledge is most fundamentally realized and expressed. Such a theoretical outlook has been developed in our own time by Emmanuel Levinas. In his conception of ethics as 'first philosophy', again a radical claim is made that all wisdom, human and divine, reduces in the end to an ethical knowing or unknowing.

It will be instructive for readers of Dante to glimpse the philosophical depths that ethical reflection can sound as it is practiced by Levinas. Beyond the sentiments involved and magisterially expressed by the poet, ethical vision constitutes an original access to truth of the kind that Dante wishes to impart. The benefits, furthermore, of this comparison are reciprocal. Dante's example helps to render palpable and compelling some far-reaching motivations for ethical vision that Levinas tends to overlook or exclude. A number of Levinas scholars have felt that his stringently ethical thinking is lacking in a cosmological and aesthetic sensibility, and they have wished to integrate his ethics with these other dimensions of knowledge and experience.[3] Something of the kind – some kind of mediation between ethics and ontology and artistic creation – can be found in full flower in Dante: he thereby helps us to imagine how a fully fleshed-out universe might be integrated into an ethical perspective, even where Levinas himself was not able or willing to pursue such a comprehensive synthesis.

This particular comparison, then, is especially illuminating because Levinas seems to be so lacking in the cosmic-aesthetic dimension of ethical vision that is so powerfully and vividly elaborated by Dante. Conversely, the deeper philosophical motivations for Dante's vision as a rigorously ethical vision are not readily apparent without explicit philosophical meditation on the meaning of ethical vision, and this is what Levinas supplies with exceptionally penetrating insight. Preliminarily, let it be said that the essence of ethics for both authors is a radical transcendence of oneself in relation to an Other who is other than all one can say. This relation is constituted in language, but specifically as its limit-condition and as manifest in the failure of language to adequately represent or express this unapproachable, inappropriable otherness.

In their different idioms, both Dante and Levinas tell of an experience of radical transcendence that reduces the individual subject to an absolute passivity and passion vis-à-vis what is characterized as not characterizable at all. Both find themselves face to face with the Ineffable. Their angles of approach to this ultimate experience of transcendence are very different: Dante's universal cosmological journey of consciousness culminates in the vision of God, whereas Levinas's effort is primarily aimed at acknowledging the claim made by the particular other person facing one as a limitless obligation of unconditional responsibility. Nevertheless, crucial aspects of what I am calling ethical vision can be brought into focus by comparing these two very different ethical visionaries. It is specifically the dimension of the ineffable as the final, inarticulable, ethical burden of language that can be made to stand out clearly by this convergence.

Dante's *Paradiso* dramatically stages the undoing of the constructive metaphysics of the *Divine Comedy* as a whole. The project of a total interpretation of the universe runs up against its limit and falters. Opening metaphysics in the direction of an apophatic theology that recognizes God as ineffable and as manifest precisely in the experience of language's *failure* brings the *Paradiso* close to various postmodern modes of thinking particularly of transgression. Paradoxically, 'transgression' can become the ultimate ethical act, requiring transcendence of every order of being that can be said and comprehended. Both Dante and Levinas conceive of ethics in inevitably transgressive terms as a transcending of every possible legitimating order in opening beyond all rule or measure to an ineffable Other.

Levinas distinguishes himself as the pre-eminent contemporary thinker of ethical encounter with absolute otherness as unsayable and yet as a pre-verbal Saying (*le Dire*), an opening and offering of self before anything whatsoever that can be Said (*le Dit*). In these characteristic concerns, he happens to match Dante's undertaking in the *Paradiso* of a journey to an encounter with an absolute Other on the basis of a Saying that obsessively courts Unsayability. Such is the ineffable divine instance that is the ultimate concern of his poem. Levinas can thus illuminate the specifically ethical motives for this unsayability that is the enabling condition, as well as the limit, of Dante's whole venture in the *Paradiso*.

Paradiso as the trace of the other

In the last canto of the *Divine Comedy*, *Paradiso* XXXIII, very near the culmination of his journey, Dante describes his mental state as resembling that of one awaking from sleep, still filled with the feeling of what he has been envisioning in dream, although the vision itself has vanished. He can no longer say for sure what, if anything, it was that shook and stirred and left him in such a state of ravishment. Still, he senses that he has been profoundly affected by something.

> *Qual è colui che somniando vede,*
> *che dopo il sogno la passione impressa*
> *rimane, e l'altro a la mente non riede,*
> *cotal son io, ché quasi tutta cessa*
> *mia visione, e ancor mi distilla*
> *nel core il dolce che nacque da essa.*
> (XXXIII.58–63)

> Like one who dreaming sees,
> upon whom after dreaming a passion is left
> impressed, while the rest does not return to mind,
> so am I, since my vision almost completely
> ceases, and still in my heart there continues to be distilled
> the sweetness that was born of it.

The passion impressed upon him remains and distills a sweetness in his heart. Yet this is only something that he feels and nothing that he sees, nor can he even remember anything of what he now calls his 'vision'. Whatever it was that presumably occasioned the passion has slipped from memory and left 'almost' (*quasi*) no trace – nothing, it seems, apart from this passion itself. The speaker is left with no distinct image of any object but with only an impression, a feeling (*passione*) that has been aroused in him by contact with what, for all that he can now ascertain, may never have existed in any objective form at all. When we wake up from a dream, as in Dante's simile, we see that what we took to be realities were in fact nothing but figments of our fantasy.

What Dante is able to recount of his 'vision' depends exclusively on what we might call the 'subjective correlative', the affective state induced in him, for that is all that can be described or even, at this stage, be retained in memory.[4] This state is felt to be correlative to an experience of something else besides itself, something other, indeed something so radically other that it cannot be expressed at all or even be remembered. The transformation wrought in Dante and the state of exaltation it induced make reference to something beyond themselves yet irretrievably lost. Dante is incapable of recapturing whatever it is that he has experienced. This reference, therefore, remains necessarily indeterminate. The subjective state induced is inherently referential, but it refers to what is simply 'other' than all that can be articulated. This state can be interpreted precisely as a 'trace' in the sense defined by Levinas.[5] To this extent, the subjective state itself becomes, in effect, the origin of the poem and its vision, at least insofar as the latter can be communicated.

The same structure of inference from a subjective, purely emotional residue that becomes the origin of all possibility of representation repeats itself a few lines later, still within the frame of the ascent toward the poem's final 'vision':

> La forma universal di questo nodo
> credo ch' i' vidi, perché più di largo,
> dicendo questo, mi sento ch' i' godo.
> (XXXIII.91–3)
> The universal form of this knot
> I believe I saw, because in saying this,
> I feel that I enjoy more amply.

Again, Dante's belief about what he saw, for which he retains no memory of any actual object as having been present, is based on what he feels, a feeling of delight in dilation when he says that he saw what he now imagines and articulates in his poem – the universal form of this 'knot' or complex unity reflected in itself. This is indeed the whole universe, substance and accidents and their modes conflated together in the simple light of divinity (XXXIII.88–90). This feeling is produced in conjunction with a present act of speech and in the absence of any actual object of vision. The way he feels now in saying it vouches for the validity of his belief as to what he saw then. In this way, the 'vision' of the poem is projected backwards from the fulfillment experienced in the *language* of vision.

The same pattern of inference, in different forms, can be found elsewhere in the *Paradiso*, indeed everywhere else, for it structures the poem in its entirety. For example, in the heaven of Mars, when Dante beholds Beatrice, or more exactly the light of divinity reflected in Beatrice, her surpassing beauty constrains him to despair of describing it, for what he sees is ineffable, but he nevertheless expounds upon what he feels, that is, his 'affect', in correlation with this indescribable beauty:

> Io mi rivolsi a l'amoroso suono
> del mio conforto; e qual io allor vidi
> ne li occhi santi amor, qui l'abbandono;

> non perch'io pur del mio parlar diffidi,
> ma per la mente che non può reddire
> sovra sé tanto, s'altri non la guidi.
> Tanto poss'io di quel punto ridire,
> che, rimirando lei, lo mio affetto
> libero fu da ogne altro disire,
> fin che 'l piacere etterno, che diretto
> raggiava in Beatrice, dal bel viso
> mi contentava col secondo aspetto.
> (XVIII.7–18)
> I turned towards the amorous sound
> coming from my comfort; and what love I then
> saw in her holy eyes, I abandon [the attempt to say];
> not only because I distrust my speech,
> but because of memory, which cannot return
> so high above itself, unless another guide it.
> So much of that moment [or point] can I retell,
> that, intently looking at her, my affections
> were free from every other desire,
> while the eternal loveliness radiantly
> shining on Beatrice contented me with
> its reflection in her beautiful eyes.

What is indescribable here is not really Beatrice's beautiful face but rather the unconditioned, the transcendent that appears therein and is represented here as a point of light (as also in XXVIII.16 and 41). The eternal beauty, or more literally 'pleasure' (*piacere etterno*), that is reflected in Beatrice's holy eyes is perhaps not a possible object of actual vision at all until it is represented as such by Dante, in correlation with the sense of satisfaction it procures him. Here again, Dante's vision in paradise, specifically of the glory that according to *Paradiso* I.1–3 in fact radiates throughout the universe, can be described only indirectly by its effects upon the emotions of the poem's speaker. In itself, what is referred to is simply and purely other than all that can be described, as is confirmed by its inaccessibility to memory, unless memory be guided by something or someone who is designated merely as 'another' (*s'altri non la guidi*). Description of what is objectively indescribable in terms of the subjective state that contact with it induces in the author constitutes the general charter for all that Dante writes about paradise, from the very first verses and throughout. The premise of the whole poem is that Dante has 'been in' the highest heaven, the Empyrean, beyond the physical universe, and has beheld the divine essence. But he cannot express or even remember what he has 'seen'.

> *Nel ciel che più de la sua luce prende*
> *fu' io, e vidi cose che ridire*
> *né sa né può chi di là sú discende* . . . .
> (I.4–6)
> (In the heaven that receives the most of his light
> I was, and I saw things which whoever descends from there
> neither knows how nor is permitted to retell . . . .)

Here at the outset of the poem Dante declares that he is conditioned by a multiplex ineffability: neither has he been able to comprehend and so remember what he 'saw' nor would he be able to express it in words even if he had. As the 'Letter to Can Grande' comments about this passage, 'he does not know [what to express] because he forgets, and he is not able [to express it] because even if he remembers and retains the content, speech nevertheless fails' (*nescit quia oblitus, nequit quia, si recordatur et contentum tenet, sermo tamen deficit*, sec. 83). The redundancy of these reasons given for the ineffability of the vision of paradise is one hint that it does not admit of any simple explanation. Its ineffability will turn out to be more essential and mysterious than anything that could simply be narrated – more a condition of (im)possibility of the narration of paradise than just one aspect or item among others *within* the narrative.[6]

Just a few verses after the opening statement of ineffability that frames the whole poem, the poet reaffirms, in an invocation to Apollo, the subjective or phantasmatic character of his account of paradise with an incisive image. He declares that he cannot relate paradise as such but can only manifest the shadow of it incised in his head (*che l'ombra del beato regno/segnata nel mio capo io manifesti* . . . , I.22-4). That is to say, he can only convey an effect that has been wrought upon him, the impression that has been scored in his memory, by an encounter with what cannot itself be represented as such – God himself and, more generally, the whole blessed realm of paradise consisting essentially in nothing other than God's presence or proximity.

I am emphasizing that Dante underscores the 'subjective' mediation of paradise – at one point he even calls it '*my* paradise' (*il mio paradiso*, XV.36) – as it is represented and made present in his poem. But it must equally be stressed that Dante always seeks and finds objective expression for his experience.[7] He uses the most objective forms of culture, especially 'scientific' and mathematical culture, available to him in order to offer 'objective correlatives' for all the feelings that he attempts to convey. Dante does not leave his exposition of personal experience at the level of merely intimistic romantic confessions. On the contrary, hard-edged, geometric images define his vision as he relates it in the *Paradiso*, markedly towards its beginning (e.g. in the use of optics to explain moon spots in Canto II) and at its end, with the reference to the geometer attempting to square the circle (*Qual è 'l geomètra* . . . XXXIII.133).

Yet the fact remains that these terms and theories are used as metaphors for an experience that itself eludes all objective accounts and is not even experience of an object (nor perhaps is it truly experience by a subject). Their 'objectivity' consists not in their corresponding to an empirically given, or even possible, object but rather in the precision and coherence with which they are poetically constructed so as to take on definite, objective form in representing an ineffable one-knows-not-what. Whatever it is that they endeavour in vain to convey remains in itself irreducibly beyond expression and objectification. It cannot be properly signified by words but requires rather a first-person experience of 'transhumanization' on the part of whoever is going to succeed in understanding the experience of paradise that Dante, from the very first canto, categorically renounces describing through adequate verbal representation:

> Trasumanar significar per verba
> non si poría; però l'essemplo basti
> a cui esperienza grazia serba.
> (I.70–2)
> Transhumanizing cannot be signified by words;
> so let the example suffice for the one
> for whom grace reserves the experience.

Thus the rhetoric of objective vision of determinate forms, however intensively and emphatically Dante employs it, must be interpreted as, strictly speaking, metaphorical. In order to give any account at all of this transcendent experience called 'paradise', Dante consistently and inevitably falls back on the portrayal of the subjective impressions that linger in him after all purportedly objective vision has vanished, and this is the immediate source of his poetry in the *Paradiso*, as he explicitly admits in passages such as those that have just been considered. It is the very relating in poetry of an experience which is in itself ineffable that objectifies 'the ineffable' in the first place. Thus, the very idea that the vision *was* a vision of an object may belong to the poetic form in which this vision is presented, more than to any original core of essential experience of the Ineffable as such. The ineffable would in this case be a poetic hypothesis, one that is found in religious and mystical representations of various sorts. It is, nonetheless, a *necessary* hypothesis, to the extent that these representations are communicated, transgressing the injunction to silence that typically surrounds and shrouds such visions. Dante's elaborating a poetry of the Ineffable would, accordingly, constitute a translation *into* representation from a radically non-representational register of contact with the Ineffable rather than just a translation *of* representations of a visual nature, whether sensible or purely spiritual, into another – a verbal – form of representation.

Witnessing to the transcendent

The poem presents itself constantly as a visionary experience, and yet the object – or, better, the sense – of that vision turns out to be beyond vision and representation. Although Dante insists on invoking the epistemological categories of vision and revelation all throughout, he is always also sensitive to the relational conditions vis-à-vis a transcendent God that circumscribe and even defeat this quest for objective knowledge. At the last moment, he always recoils from direct representation of the Godhead and assumes an attitude that needs to be understood rather as ethical in character, as an ethical stance towards what in its innermost core remains irreducibly external to representation and knowledge. The limits of knowledge and representation that he runs up against disclose to him not only his own subjectivity and its limits but also its inherent reference to what exceeds it, to what involves him passionately, even though he cannot represent it. To this he-knows-not-what he cannot help but bear witness and testify – and indeed that is all he can do. To begin to understand the poem from the specifically ethical perspective that is the ethos pervading Dante's whole *oeuvre*, as is stated explicitly with respect to the *Paradiso* by the 'Letter to Can Grande', we have an incomparable resource in the philosophical reflections of Emmanuel Levinas and the insight it opens into ethics.[8]

Levinas is an invaluable guide leading us into the inaccessible reaches of an ethical 'experience' that is, properly speaking, beyond experience and expression. His ultra-phenomenological explorations illuminate philosophically what may after all be the only possible path through the territory of the ineffable and unrepresentable, a territory that is charted also, however differently, by the *Paradiso*. The ineffable is a vast, in itself limitless realm to be explored, and Dante is one of its most original explorers. In the wake of Christian mystical tradition, he sets sail in the vessel of his poetry upon this high sea or *alto sale* (*Par.* II.1–12). His metaphysical imagery reveals itself as a metaphor for what in the end demands to be understood as an ethical relation to the unrepresentable Other – whether this be God or a significant other like Beatrice.

Levinas's thought deeply probes how the ethical remains unrepresentable because it necessarily originates in the absolutely Other – other to all that can be thought or said. Western thought, ever since its inception with Parmenides, and again in modern times with Descartes, has generally attempted to derive all that is, all being, from the Self and the Same. But whatever originates in the Self or the Same comes back around to self-interest in the end and misses the whole point of the ethical, namely, responsibility to the Other. Since I cannot represent the Other without mediating it in terms that are inevitably my own, I cannot represent the absolutely or wholly other (*le tout autre*). There is no phenomenon that can make manifest, or any words that can represent, this sort of contact. I can, however, represent my obsession with this Other. Its bearing upon me and its binding me in infinite obligation can genuinely be 'experienced', which means simply that such an ethical conviction can be irresistibly produced in me. And on this basis, then, representations, not of the Other but of its effects on me, can and indeed do proliferate. This is what, according to Levinas, engenders the ethical subject, the core of 'the me' (*le moi*), in its uniqueness. This originary contact with the Other that actually engenders the ethical human subject belongs to a past that is never present and to a passivity more passive than that of any subject because it is before the 'I' that can act or fail to act or even be conscious of itself and its freedom as an autonomous agent: relation to the Other is the precondition of all these forms and faculties of ethical selfhood.

What Dante offers in the *Paradiso* is, in Levinas's terms, witness or 'testimony' to the vision of God in Paradise, the indescribable experience that is described as one of being directly present in and to the divine. Dante testifies to the effects on him of an 'experience' that defies representation. Even to call it experience is not quite correct. It can best be understood as belonging to a pre-experiential order consisting in unrecognizable, unrealizable relatedness, specifically relation to an absolute Other, before we can even be aware of ourselves as ourselves or of the Other as other. This is the 'before', the antecedent, of all human experience that Levinas elucidates in ethical terms. Experience tends to posit an experiential subject with an identity, whereas the ethical relation with the Other (and at this stage it is not possible even to distinguish between the Other as the other person and as God) is anterior to all self-aware experience and self-identity. To encounter the Other in its otherness, one must be radically undone as a self, deprived of the structures of self-relation that close out the absolutely other by appropriating and defining everything else in the self's own terms.

The Other is not a phenomenon that I can perceive and process, though I am ethically aware of being in relation to this Other – of my obligation to be concerned for this Other and ethically to put the Other first. And while I cannot represent the Other, I can testify to it through my response of recognizing my ethical responsibility for the Other as prior to my own constitution as a self. In this way, the Other is not known but is rather acknowledged as residing at the very core and origin of my own being and identity as a subject. Dante's poem is such a response to the Other, to the Other ultimately as God, and it registers Dante's 'experience' of God by the effects that this divine Other has upon Dante. The effects are constitutive of Dante's subjectivity by the destruction of all his own constructions of himself, laying him open in infinite vulnerability to the invasion of otherness. For Levinas, this passion of the subject is the only way that the contact with the Other, given its transcendence, can be made manifest. And precisely this passion is to be found at the heart of Dante's poem. Indeed, it is this passion of the subject speaking in accents of a bold new individuality that assumes in Dante's poetic reenactment of the Christ event the centrality that we would otherwise expect to be reserved for the Passion. This may explain why direct representation of the drama of Christ's Passion is conspicuously absent from the poem, being only alluded to and recalled symbolically.[9]

Whatever Dante may actually hear and see, the ethical core of his experience of the otherness of God must necessarily be guarded in blind silence, as the poem continually attests. Levinas is the modern thinker who has made most clear that testimony of this order refers to what is prior to all appearing and manifestation. He explains how in testimony it is impossible to go behind the response to what provokes it (except blindly by faith). The only observable phenomenon is the response itself. That to which it is a response does not and cannot present itself, though it has occasioned and apparently compelled the response. The appeal of the Transcendent – what transcends every possibility of representation and expression – is first heard in the response. Levinas accordingly undertakes to explain '... that the call is heard in the response, that the "provocation" coming from God is in my invocation, that gratitude is already gratitude for this state of gratitude, which would be, at once or by turns, gift and gratitude' (... *que l'appel s'y entend dans la réponse, que la 'provocation' venant de Dieu est dans mon invocation, que la gratitude est déjà gratitude pour cet état de gratitude qui serait, à la fois ou tour à tour, le don et la gratitude*, Autrement qu'être, p. 234).

Stemming from biblical roots, the pattern of relationship that Levinas conceptualizes here is common in Christian mystical approaches to God.[10] God's address to humans is discerned in and as the human invocation of God, where the invocation itself is ambiguously the source of the divine presence – a paradox from which Augustine begins and on which the entire discourse of the *Confessions* is predicated. This effects a reversal in which response becomes originary – at least insofar as any possible manifestation, any presentation or representation, is concerned. Yet, at the same time, Levinas stresses that response is precisely *not* its own origin, for it originates in the Other – beyond or before representation. This is a past that was never present because it cannot be manifest, and so happen, at all. It is always already past, 'older' than every past that was ever present. Still, it belongs to the originary structure of any possibility of representation to a subject and therefore of any experience in the present.

I have already suggested that Levinas has made possible a deep philosophical understanding of why ethics necessarily has its grounds in what cannot be represented. The Other in its radical otherness can never be attained by representation, for representation always circles back to the Self and the Same. To *re*-present is to assimilate and appropriate into a framework that cannot recognize the Other except as a species of the Same. Representation remains within the activity of a self presenting its world to itself in terms commensurate with itself and therefore confined within the circle of its autonomy and egotism. The ethical recognition of the otherness of the Other must break away precisely from any and all such systems of self-reference. And to do so, it must move beyond representation to what Levinas calls 'signification'.

Levinas describes a wholly other kind of signification than that based on reference to visible (or otherwise appearing and thematizable) objects in the indifference and distance of simply 'knowing' them. It is a kind of signification born rather of contact and even obsession. This kind of signification he calls 'transcending', and he designates it as the significance of signification itself. It is what renders signification in the ordinary sense possible:

> Not to be able to stay within a theme, not to be able to appear – this invisibility which makes itself 'contact' and obsession, stems not from the insignificance of that which is approached, but from a way of signifying that is wholly other than that which binds ostention to vision: here, beyond visibility, what is exposed is not any signification that would still be thematized in the sign; it is *transcending* itself of this same beyond that is signification. Signification, that is to say, the contradictory trope of the *one for the other*.

> *Ne pas pouvoir tenir dans un theme, ne pas pouvoir apparaître – cette invisibilité qui se fait 'contact' et obession, tient non pas à l'insignifiance de ce qui est approché, mais à une façon de signifier toute autre que celle qui relie ostention à vision: ici, au-delà de la visibilité ne s'expose aucune signification qui serait encore thématisée dans son signe ; c'est le transcender même de cet au-delà qui est signification. Signification, c'est-à-dire le trope contradictoire de l'un-pour-l'autre'.* (Autrement qu'être, p. 158)

The originary sense of signification is transcending. That means transcending all that can be thematically signified by a sign. But as a relation to something other, the sign is not simply what it is or even what it thematically signifies. It opens beyond itself towards an Other. What it is emerges through and cannot be abstracted from what it signifies in this sense of transcending all thematic signification. Signification in this sense involves a substitution of the one for the other, as in the basic structure of signification (A for B). Such substitution has an ethical sense and is accomplished in the ethical passion of responsibility, of being 'for the other' in one's ownmost being, in the very act, or rather passion, by which one is constituted as 'one'. All human significance comes from transcending the self towards the Other to whom one is ethically responsible before one is even conscious of being oneself, of being one – for this ethical responsibility vis-à-vis an Other is the bond that first makes a human being individual and 'one'. Nothing means or signifies anything humanly outside of this indispensable condition of all significance, namely, one's ethical responsibility for the Other. This alone anchors values of whatever kind and gives them human significance – if the human is to be anything more than raw egotism. This originary or rather pre-originary relatedness to the Other is what Levinas calls the ethical, for it means that we are bound by obligation to the Other before we are 'ourselves' at all and as a condition of our becoming conscious of ourselves as individuals.

Levinas's central claim is that sense or significance does not proceed from essence (*Autrement qu'être*, p. 271). Things' and persons' meanings are not determined by what they essentially are. On the contrary, the sense of all beings proceeds from their relation to the Other. Being, as a system of essences with identities, is relativized by the ethical demand that comes from the Other. This is a philosophy in which sense – significance *for* someone – precedes being and essence. The sense of my being *for* you, the one for the other, comes ethically before any determinations of being or essence. It is not because of what I *am* that I give myself to others. This would lead me back ineluctably into the circle of self-interest. The sense of the one as for the other, unconditionally, must come first, before having any essence in and for oneself, since this sense comes from the Other and ignores all dictates of being, evades any identity and transgresses all supposed guidelines or laws of essence. To this degree, the self cannot but be absolutely passive vis-à-vis the

Other: any activity would be an appropriation of the Other by the self that would allow it no longer to be wholly other. This uncompromising orientation towards the Other is what Levinas conceives as 'otherwise than being and beyond essence'. Its sense is transgressive of the regime of being and essence.

Now Dante's whole poem, not least in its impassioned pleas for justice on earth, is an attempt to describe the passion whereby he becomes possessed by the Other as 'God'. In the failure of its descriptions, the poem illustrates the passivity in which he is affected by the Other at the very core of and indeed before the origin of his being. Dante's own profoundest reality is that of the Infinite, and it is thus wholly incommensurable with any humanly definable identity. Just as Augustine had found God to be more interior than his own self (*interior meo*, *Confessiones* III.vi.11), so Dante transcends himself towards an infinite and unknowable God at every stage of his journey through Paradise. The poem is nothing but a series of rehearsals of this motion of transcendence, which is registered on Dante's sensibility as exceeding his capacities ever anew. It is the search for – and thereby the discovery and manifestation of – a signification that cannot be expressed *per verba*. This transcendence beyond essence and identity comes closer to Levinas's understanding of metaphysics than to the usual textbook Scholastic metaphysics of Dante's own time.

In Levinas's language, Dante's 'I' is affected by the Infinite and Transcendent. The whole of the *Paradiso* testifies to the Divine in terms of its effects upon the subject who says 'I' in the poem. Yet what it is that affects the speaker cannot be represented or spoken. He can only give an account of the ethical relation of being beholden to the Other – as witnessed to by the obsession it has inspired in him. Given this condition, all the metaphors of the poem, in the guise of metaphysical revelations, are determined fundamentally as metaphors for this ethical sense, which is itself referred to something that – or rather someone who – remains as such unrepresentable.

While the Transcendent cannot as such appear, it is irresistible and imperious and indeed operates as an imperative in opening up a realm of revelation and representation for the one who has come into contact with it. The poem is the witness to what it is not, to the Transcendent that has passed through the subject's experience, leaving the subject in effect traumatized, at the same time as it constitutes the ethical subject in the first place. This is, after all, the traditional structure of witness and testimony as it is found in the words of the Bible. What so profoundly affects and changes people in their lives and hearts is not objectifiable. It is only the *effect* of such traumatic affecting that can be expressed: such is the nature of revelation in religious experience. It is patent, for example, in the testimony provided by the Gospels to Jesus as the Son of God – as worker of miracles and as resurrected from the dead, where the emphasis falls always on the extraordinary effects upon the witnesses to events which themselves remain recalcitrant to representation. The same can be said of the Exodus – specifically of God's appearance shrouded in smoke and lightning during the theophany at Sinai (Exodus 19–20).

Levinas's thinking can illuminate aspects of the ethical that have been operative in representations of religious revelation all through Western tradition, particularly in the wake of the Bible, but which have never before been elucidated philosophically with such penetration. His thinking suggests that what religious revelation reveals fundamentally is the transcendence of the Other. The ethical Other is infinite and in effect divine: one is obligated to the Other without reservation or limit. At this level of absoluteness, the ethical relations to God and to one's neighbour tend to coincide. The primary reference of Dante's ethical relation in the *Paradiso* is God, whereas for Levinas it is in the first instance the neighbour, but the same dissymmetry and infinite responsibility or obligation apply in either case. Indeed the two relations – to God and to neighbour – are for both authors and their respective traditions deeply inseparable. They are different registers of representation for contact with an unrepresentable otherness.

For Levinas, the ethical is experienced in the approach to the radically other and inassimilable, the Other that remains irreducibly external to the sphere of conscious experience and its phenomena. This relation Levinas calls 'proximity', and it is enacted by Dante's asymptotic nearing of the desired goal of his journey alluded to from the poem's opening sentence: 'drawing near to its desire' (*appressandosi al suo desire*, I.7), as well as in its concluding canto: 'And I, who was nearing the end of all desires' (*e io ch'al fine di tutti disii/appropinquava*, XXXIII.46–7). The God that is beyond all objective experience and inexpressible can, so far as any discourse is concerned, only be *approached*: the whole poem is but an approach to God. Even in the final vision of the last canto, it is only the nearing and not the union itself that can be consciously experienced and described. In this dimension of proximity, the Other cannot be apprehended directly as an object but only in and through desire and the other affects engendered in the subject.

For all the resources he deploys, borrowed especially from Christian mystical tradition, in order to burrow into the light of God that penetrates the whole universe in diverse degrees, Dante winds up offering a striking testimony to the ultimate impossibility of penetrating the divine essence – and so to its status as irreducibly other to human experience and comprehension. In 'figuring' paradise he is forced to jump 'like one who finds his path cut off' (*come chi trova suo cammin riciso*, XXIII. 61–3). The poem's constant emphasis on impasses to writing and even to remembering this impossible 'experience' of transcending the human (*trasumanar*) witnesses to Dante's awareness of the constitutive non-representability of his encounter with what is radically inassimilable and indescribable – 'ineffabile', in Dante's code word. The modes of subjective experience to which Dante makes recourse are precisely those of witness, testimony and obsession, and Levinas's philosophical exposition of these terms illuminates crucial aspects of Dante's poem as a fundamentally ethical journey of approach to the unknowable Other. At its deepest level, the content of Dante's representations cannot but be read as illustrating the kind of radical ethics of the unrepresentable and inexpressible contact with otherness around which all Levinas's thinking revolves.

As we have already begun to see, the effects upon the subject of its ethical contact with the unknowable and inexpressible, which is the ethical Other, whether the absolute Other in the sense of God or simply the absolute of the other person, are described by Levinas in terms of 'obsession', 'trauma' and, of course, 'desire'. These are indeed the states that are most apt to describe Dante's subjective experience in the *Paradiso* as symbolized, for example, by Semelè at the beginning of Canto XXI: destroyed as a result of insisting that Jove, her lover, show himself to her, Semelè is recalled to illustrate how Dante could be incinerated by the complete unveiling of the (to him) intolerably intense radiance of Beatrice's smile. In heaven, in the approach to the Face of God, even triumphs can be traumatic. The work presents an anatomy of Dante's obsessions and traumas. These are expressed in terms of all the modes of a sensibility that strains and falters in responding to what exceeds the bounds of the knowable. And this is what becomes the real revelation of the poem as a witness to what cannot be represented.

The effects of contact with the Other on the Self testify to the 'Other in me', which Levinas describes as 'sensibility': 'the being acted upon of sensibility beyond its capacity to be acted upon – which describes the suffering and vulnerability of the sensible as the *other-in-me*...' (*le subir de la sensibilité au-delà de sa capacité de subir – ce qui décrit la souffrance et la vulnérabilité du sensible comme l'autre-en-moi*..., *Autrement qu'être*, p. 198). It is my vulnerability to suffering as a sensible creature that makes me open to being affected externally. My embodied condition is not added on, but is rather the way I am constituted originally as openness or exposure to the Other. Before anything definable in terms of consciousness, I *am* my vulnerability to being hurt, and the immediacy of my bodily existence exposed externally is the sign of this. Humanly and ethically, I am constituted by the exposure to and responsibility for the Other. Levinas calls this 'incarnation'.

In the *Paradiso* Dante's senses and what they suffer become the sign of God, that is, of the Other-in-me. This is curious, since he is in Paradise and presumably beyond sense experience – although this is rigorously so only in Cantos XXX.37–XXXIII.145, in the Empyrean, which alone is 'paradise' in the strictest sense. Nonetheless, it is precisely sensibility which opens the beyond-being, the ethical 'region' beyond the phenomenal universe of the manifestation of beings, and this is what *Paradiso* in a deep sense is about. Although it is questionable whether his body can be present in the heavens, the poem expresses his experience constantly in terms of the bodily senses and of a wealth of natural sights and sounds right from the first canto: lightning sparks and flowing water and leaping fire. The senses are necessary to express metaphorically the sort of proximity and susceptibility that contact with the Other entails. Dante leaves unresolved the question of whether he really experiences Paradise (at least up to the Empyrean) with his physical senses, in his body or without it: 'Whether I was only that which you created/newly, you alone, Love, who govern heaven, know' (*S'i era sol de me quel che creasti / novellamente, amor che 'l ciel governi, tu 'l sai . . .*, I.73–5). In this, he echoes Saint Paul, who writes that he was 'caught up into paradise', 'whether in the body or out of the body, I cannot tell: God knoweth' (II Corinthians 12.3–2). But in any case, sensibility is the indispensable metaphor for this experience of proximity to the Other that affects one beyond one's ability to know and apprehend it.

As is highlighted by a plethora of intense images of excessive sensation, Dante's journey in the *Paradiso* is a radical *un*grounding of self in the search for an origin in transcendence. Only in the face of the Other, God, is Dante anything at all. Every stage of the journey traumatizes him and 'unselfs' him a degree further. Indeed, a self constituted intrinsically by relation to an Other cannot be anything in and for itself. Its being comes to it only as a result of this relation. It must orient itself otherwise than by the presumed truth of Being and the givenness of beings. It is before all else subject to the ethical imperative of the Other first: 'Après vous, Monsieur' ('After you, Sir'), as Levinas puts it in disarmingly simple, colloquial terms. Putting the Other first, before oneself, is the heart of ethics. And it implies the suspension of Being, for one's own very being must be suspended in the total abandon of self for the Other. To claim nothing for oneself, no identity, not even being itself, in order that all that one is be given from and to the Other – such is the radical ethical challenge discerned by Levinas through phenomenological reflection but also on the basis of the ethical vision and call of the Bible, particularly as announced by the prophets.[11] It is nothing less than the most radical transgression of the whole order of Being that is demanded by Levinasian ethics.

Ethical un-selfing of metaphysical self-building

Now Dante's notoriously self-assertive aplomb and egocentricity would seem at first to flagrantly contradict such ethical self-effacement in the face of the Other. Indeed, Dante's poem as a whole is evidently a self-staging of megalomaniac proportions. Yet the last leg of it, the *Paradiso*, undoes this whole construction, unsays the said, opens Dante's carefully constructed and strongly asserted self to an Infinity and otherness in its midst. In one of its concluding images, contiguous with the verses quoted at the outset of this essay, the very pages of the poem are depicted as coming undone and as being dispersed like the oracles that Sibyl committed to leaves that were blown about her cave by the winds, or like snow coming 'unsealed' in the sun that melts it:

> *Così la neve al sol si disigilla;*
> *così al vento ne le foglie levi*
> *si perdea la sentenza di Sibilla.*
> (XXXIII.64-6)
>
> Thus the snow under the sun comes unsealed;
> thus on light leaves in the wind
> the oracles of Sibyl were dispersed.

A few lines later, God is represented as a book in which everything that unfolds itself throughout the universe is united (85-90). In God, everything is gathered into 'one volume bound by love' (*legato con amore in un volume*, XXXIII.86). However, the metaphorical dispersion of the leaves of Dante's book signals the final unknowability to him of this God represented as the book that remains bound and that binds everything within it in the bond of love. Only a lightning flash of grace in the final lines suspends this inability of Dante to gather his experience of Godhead into one and know it. He is taken over to the side of the Other in direct contact, but this remains an aporia for his mind like the squaring of the circle for the geometer: it is not within reach for his own wings – or 'pens' (*non eran da ciò le proprie penne*, XXXIII.133-41). It is, in effect, a transcending and losing of himself in relation to the

Transcendent. This is an 'ethical' relation of transcendence in Levinas's sense, and such transcendence remains beyond Dante's powers of representation.

Dante does conceive of God as 'the great sea of being' (*il gran mar dell'essere*, I.113) upon which he journeys in order to return to his true home and origin. Yet he also feels out the limits of this structure and intimates that it passes into its opposite. For he must lose this being in order to find it again, and this is what all the passions suffered in the overwhelming sensory experience of the *Paradiso* are finally about. They reduce Dante to naught: his undoing is the necessary means of his progress. Dante is repeatedly shattered at each successive level of his ascent. He loses sight and consciousness and experiences his absolute inadequacy – *mi sento in questa/disagguaglianza* ('I feel myself in this inequality', XV.83) – vis-à-vis his heavenly interlocutors. The opening of Canto XXV imagines Dante's return to Florence with quite another appearance (*con altra voce omai, con altro vello*) than that with which he left his native city. It registers the poet's sense of his having become irreversibly other by aging – an irreversibility that is likewise a major pivot of Levinas's theory of diachronicity as structural openness to the Other in *Totalité et infini*.

Dante's *Paradiso* surely is a song of the self, and the journey it recounts is nothing if not an apotheosis of the self. But at every stage, Dante encounters the limits and the groundlessness of this same self, for its ground is in a God that is so radically other as to be incapable of being described or comprehended by the self. To this extent, the self's own origin is in otherness. Dante's pilgrimage is a return home, but it is a return to an unknown, never before experienced 'home' in the otherness of God, and to this extent it is a being at home in exile. This was Dante's historical and intimate experience as an individual, and it is reflected in the language he created, especially in its culminating form in the *Paradiso*. The poem's ideology remains one of return to one's own, to a God to whom one belongs, but if we heed Dante's insistent declarations of the impossibility of his task in the *Paradiso* – as we must – it is clear how this reconciliation of self and other is leveraged from the

Other and the unknown. 'God' is the truth of the self who can never truly know itself except in the God who transcends knowledge.

Levinas insists on the 'beyond' of being because everything in the system of manifestations of being presupposes an identity that is not totally dependent upon and beholden to the Other. Being, with its essences, posits a foundation in self-identity and thus in an egoism that rules out radical ethical responsibility from the start. Only by starting from the Other can ethics, or responsibility, in the basic sense of 'the one for the other', or of 'I-responsible-for-you', emerge. For being in its self-sufficiency and autotelic self-enclosedness is essentially opposed to the openness of passion towards the Other as the first moment and movement of what, before being, is in the process of becoming a subject. On the way to responsible personhood, to which it is called by the Other, the subject as yet has no essential identity in and for itself. Levinas calls this pre-originary or 'an-archic' im-personality '*illéité*'.

Now Dante certainly thinks within the philosophy of being and essence as he found it in the Scholastic philosophers and theologians and especially in Thomas Aquinas, for whom God was Being itself (*esse ipsum*). And yet in his writing he presses this conception to an extreme where it tends to collapse into its opposite. The whole metaphysical construction is turned inside out by its emergent ethical sense. In Dante's poetic rendition, pivoting from his addresses to the reader, the *significance* of theological doctrine *for* the one who receives it, rather than just its doctrinal content or supposedly objective truth, becomes paramount, and this significance is ethical. The *Paradiso* is in this regard the capstone of Dante's whole project of vulgarizing theology and philosophy, translating Latin learning into the vernacular.

Prima facie Dante's poem, as a pillar of Western metaphysical and mystical tradition, seems to be the epitome of all that Levinas's thought aims to challenge and dismantle. Dante offers a totalizing representation of the whole order of Being. He is thoroughly immersed in the vocabulary of essences and identities. The new Scholastic language and vision are among the materials fundamental for his poem. Yet in the *Paradiso* he also exposes a gap inherent in this system of Being. He exposes the system as based on what itself has no definable identity or knowable essence, on what can only be testified to as beyond all possibility of representation. In Dante's poem, being and knowledge show themselves to be metaphors for something else, something other, something ultimately of an irreducibly ethical character. Thus, the poem illustrates how the critique of the metaphysical, ontological tradition is already active within its own bosom, at the very heart of its inspiration. In effect, the poem brings out the negative, apophatic theology that necessarily conditions all genuine theological epiphany and metaphysical revelation. This emphasis is the constant message and general posture of the *Paradiso*. It constitutes a reply *avant la lettre* to a prevalent postmodern rejection of metaphysics, recalling that the rejection was already anticipated in the original assertion because that very assertion of a total system of being is itself motivated by a relation to the Other that is beyond Being. This comes out clearly in the self-declared impossible attempt of writing the *Paradiso*. It also suggests that in order to go beyond Being, one must not simply suppress Being. Being is what one needs in order to 'go beyond'. This is what Dante's poem, as a celebration of being in a self-transcending song of the self, in effect demonstrates.

It must be admitted (and has been) at another and much more obvious level that Dante stands rather for the antithesis of Levinas's ideas. In terms of the fiction of his narration, Dante proposes a metaphysical vision founded on the direct intuition of the divine essence. He expresses this consistently as a seeing. I do not wish to diminish the importance of this form of expression for Dante. In Canto II (as again at the poem's end), he defines his driving motivation as the desire to see 'that essence in which is seen how our nature is united with God' (*il disio/di veder quella essenza in che si vede/come nostra natura e Dio s'unìo*), and he indicates that there, at his journey's end in God's presence, this divine essence will be immediately 'seen', without demonstration, as a primary truth:

> *Lì si vedrà ciò che tenem per fede,*
> *non dimostrato, ma fia per sé noto*
> *a guisa del ver primo che l'uom crede.*
> (II.40–5)

> There one will see what we hold by faith,
> not demonstrated, but self-evident
> like the first truth that man believes.

Nevertheless, this way of imagining the contact with the divine does not prevent Dante from exploring in essentially ethical terms a 'vision' which cannot actually be seen, as he relentlessly reminds us, except perhaps in the very failure of the representations of his poetry. The vision in this sense remains a theological hypothesis that serves, narratively, as a mythic scaffolding for the ethical revelation worked out concretely by the poet in the language of the poem with its impassioned political content and urgent moral message. In this way, Dante's final work assumes a transgressive dimension of otherness with respect to its own and every possible representation that makes his poetry profoundly contemporary with the postmodern age. This enables it also to expose – together with Levinas, a postmodern prophet of transcendence in an ethical sense – what is so lacking in our own age, which has become practically immune to all the nevertheless irrepressible testimonials of 'transcendence' in its midst.

Notes

Introduction

1 This has been effectively emphasized by Zygmunt Baranski, for example, in 'The Roots of Dante's Plurilingualism: "Hybridity" and Language in the *Vita nova*', in *Dante's Plurilingualism, Authority, Knowledge, Subjectivity*, eds S. Fortuna, M. Gragnolati, and J. Trabant (Oxford: Legenda, 2010): 'Dante was eager to experiment by "transgressively" amalgamating different "styles"' (p. 101); 'as is well known, in Dante, the "trangressive" mixing of the *stili* is considered the supreme expression of his literary inventiveness' (p. 99).

2 Epistles VI and XI, respectively. Dante's 'minor' works are cited from *Opere minori*, 2 vols, eds A. Frugoni, F. Brugnoli, et al. (Milan: Ricciardi, 1979–88). The *Comedy* is cited from *La Divina Commedia secondo l'antica vulgata*, ed. Giorgio Petrocchi, 4 vols (Milan: Mondadori, 1966–67).

3 René Guénon, *L'ésoterisme de Dante* (Paris: Gallimard, 1957 [1925]), Eugène Aroux, *Dante hérétique, révolutionnaire et socialiste* (Paris: Niclaus, 1939 [1854]), D. G. Rossetti, *La Beatrice di Dante: Ragionamenti critici* (London: Rossetti, 1842), Luigi Valli, *Il linguaggio segreto di Dante e dei 'Fedeli d'Amore* (Genova: Dioscuri,1988 [1922]), Giovanni Pascoli, *Minerva oscura: La costruzione morale del poema di Dante* (Milan: Pafpo, 1998 [1898]).

4 Alexis Ladame, *Dante, Prophète d'un monde uni* (Paris: Grancher, 1996). Gian Maria Ferretto, *Dante e Nostradamus: L'enigma della lapide di Torino* (Treviso: Edizioni G.M.F., 2001).

5 The transgressiveness of Dante's Franciscanism is treated by Sergio Cristaldi, *Dante di fronte al Gioachimismo: Dalla 'Vita nova' alla 'Monarchia'* (Caltanisetta: Sciascia, 2000) and N. R. Havley, *Dante and the Franciscans: Poverty and the Papacy in the Commedia* (Cambridge: Cambridge University Press, 2004). Dante is presented as a radical Aristotelian (or Averroist) by Maria Corti, *Dante a un nuovo crocevia* (Florence: Sansoni, 1982) and by numerous scholars, including

Ernest Fortin and Paul Cantor, following the work of Miguel Asìn Palacios, *Dissidence et philosophie au moyen-âge* (Montréal: Fides, 2002), trans. Marc A. Lepain as *Dissent and Philosophy in the Middle Ages: Dante and his Precursors* (Lanham, Maryland: Lexington, 2002), and Paul A. Cantor, *The Uncanonical Dante: The Divine Comedy and Islamic Philosophy* (Baltimore: Johns Hopkins University Press, 1996), following the work of Miguel Asín Palacios, *La escatologia muslmana en la Divine Comedia* (Madrid: Real Academia Española, 1919).

6 If comprehensiveness were remotely possible, I would consider also the powerful reflections on transgression by Luce Irrigaray, Julia Kristeva and Hélène Cixous. Informed by Kristeva and Lacan, Gary P. Cestaro, *Dante and the Grammar of the Nursing Body* (Notre Dame: University of Notre Dame Press, 2003) brings out the transgressiveness, for Dante's medieval culture, of the ancient figure of the nurse giving bodily nurture and thereby threatening the autonomy of the (male) self and its rationally regulated language.

7 Teodolinda Barolini, 'Arachne, Argus, and St. John: Transgressive Art in Dante and Ovid', *Mediaevalia* 13 (1987), pp. 213–16; Pamela Royston Macfie, 'Ovid, Arachne and the Poetics of *Paradiso*', in Rachel Jacoff and Jeffrey T. Schnapp, eds, *The Poetry of Allusion: Virgil and Ovid in Dante's 'Commedia'* (Stanford: Stanford University Press, 1991), pp. 159–72. The transgressive spaces of female desire opened by such figures are explored further by Rachel Jacoff, 'Transgression and Transcendence: Figures of Female Desire in Dante's *Commedia*', in *The New Medievalism*, ed. Marina S. Brownlee, Kevin Brownlee, and Stephen G. Nichols (Baltimore: Johns Hopkins University Press, 1991), pp. 183–200.

8 The commentary tradition on this point is summarized by Robert Hollander in his edition of the *Paradiso* (New York: Doubleday, 2007). Hollander's commentaries can be consulted also through the Princeton Dante Project (http://etcweb.princeton.edu/dante/pdp/) for a digest of what scholarship has established concerning each of the above-mentioned mythological personages.

9 That Dante's neologisms belong to the problematic of speaking the unspeakable is noted by Joseph Luzzi, '"As a Leaf on a Branch...": Dante's Neologisms', *PMLA* 125/2 (2010): 322–36, who stresses the

dynamism of language and the importance of neologism especially in the *Paradiso*, with its poetics of silence: 'the crux of the Dantesque neologism: its relation to language's other, silence' (p. 331).

10 Michelangelo Picone, 'Dante argonauta: La ricezione dei miti ovidiani nella *Commedia*', in *Ovidius redivivus: von Ovid zu Dante*, eds M. Picone and B. Zimmermann (Stuttgart: M&P Verlag, 1994), pp. 173-202, emphasizes Dante's differentiation and distancing of himself from the Ovidian myths he imitates (*imitatio*) by a counter-movement in which he emulates (*aemulatio*) and reformulates the same myths from a Christian moral perspective. Peter Hawkins, in chapters on 'The Metamorphosis of Ovid' and 'Transfiguring the Text' in *Dante's Testaments: Essays in Scriptural Imagination* (Stanford: Stanford University Press, 1999), finely demonstrates Dante's (dis) appropriating images from classical poetry for Christian typological purposes: metamorphosis becomes 'transfiguration'.

11 The tension between those critics intent on keeping Dante in his medieval context and those trumpeting him as the first vigorous outbreak of the modern spirit of the Renaissance – following Jacob Burkhardt – is legendary and hardly to be resolved one way or the other.

12 *Purgatorio* XXVI, with its thematics of sexual and linguistic transgression, in its sweep from the biblical Sodom and Gomorrah to amatory poets Guido Gunizzelli and Arnaut Daniel, completes the pattern.

13 '*Presumpsit ergo in corde suo incurabilis homo sub persuasione gigantis Nembroth, arte sua non solum superare naturam, sed etiam ipsum naturantem, qui Deus est*' (*De vulgari eloquenzia*, I.vii.4). 'Under the persuasion of the giant Nimrod, incorrigeable man therefore presumed in his heart to surpass by his art not only nature but even him who natures nature, who is God'.

14 The issue is taken up by Albert Russell Ascoli, *Dante and the Making of a Modern Author* (Cambridge: Cambridge University Press, 2008) and is explored indirectly by books such as María Rosa Menocal, *Writing in Dante's Cult of Truth: From Borges to Boccaccio* (Durham: Duke University Press, 1991) and Erica Durante, *Poétique et écriture: Dante au miroir de Valéry et de Borges* (Paris: H. Champion, 2008).

15 Diego Sbacchi, *La presenza di Dionigi l'Areopagita nel 'Paradiso' di Dante* (Florence: Olschki, 2006). Marco Ariani, *Lux inaccessibilis: Metafore e teologia della luce nel Paradiso di Dante* (Rome: Aracne, 2010).

Chapter 2

1 An intriguing discussion of such authorities and their influence, as well as of challenges to them, is R. Howard Bloch, *Etymologies and Genealogies: A Literary Anthropology of the French Middle Ages* (Chicago: University of Chicago Press, 1983). A good treatment of this medieval background is John M. Fyler, *Language and the Declining World in Chaucer, Dante, and Jean de Meun* (Cambridge: Cambridge University Press, 2007), chapter 1: 'The Biblical History of Language'.
2 Simone Marchesi, *Dante and Augustine: Linguistics, Poetics, Hermeneutics* (Toronto: University of Toronto Press, 2010) analyses the links between Augustine's sign theory and Dante's poetics.
3 Elena Lombardi, *The Syntax of Desire: Language and Love in Augustine, The Modistae, Dante* (Toronto: University of Toronto Press, 2007), p. 24.
4 I gather and expound exemplary passages in *On What Cannot Be Said: Apophatic Discourses in Philosophy, Religion, Literature, and the Arts* (Notre Dame: University of Notre Dame Press, 2007), vol. I: Classical Formulations.
5 For example, Giuliana Carugati, *Dalla menzogna al silenzio: La scrittura mistica della 'Commedia' di Dante* (Bologna: Il Mulino, 1991) and Manuela Colombo, *Dai mistici a Dante: Il linguaggio dell'ineffabilità* (Firenze: La Nuova Italia, 1987). See also note 15 of Chapter 1 above.
6 Massimo Baldini, 'Il mistico tra silenzio e parola', in *Le forme del silenzio e della parola*, eds M. Baldini and S. Zucal (Brescia: Morcelliana, 1989), p. 254.
7 Kevin Hart, *The Trespass of the Sign: Deconstruction, Theology and Philosophy* (Cambridge: Cambridge University Press, 1989), pp. 3–4.

8 Derrida's notion of writing as implying absence and exile has its medieval antecedents, for example, in Isidor of Seville or in Thomas Aquinas, and Dante is provocatively reversing such connotations.
9 I work this reading out in greater detail in 'Scripture as Theophany in Dante's *Paradiso*', *Religion and Literature* 39/2 (Spring 2007): 1–32.
10 R. A. Shoaf, *Dante, Chaucer and the Currency of the Word* (Norman, Oklahoma: Pilgrim Books, 1983), especially 'Narcissus and the Poet', pp. 21–38. I develop these ideas in *Self-Reflection and the Apotheosis of Lyric in Dante's Paradiso* (manuscript).

Chapter 3

1 Maurice Blanchot, *L'entretien infini* (Paris: Gallimard, 1969), p. vii.
2 Eugenio Montale, 'Discorso su Dante' (1965), in *Atti del Congresso Internazionale di Studi danteschi*, vol. II (Florence: Sansoni, 1966) sums up this typically modern view. See, further, Georg Rabuse, 'Die Ganzheitsaspekt der Philosophie bei Dante', *Zeitschrift für Ganzheitsforschung* 5 (1961): 117–24.
3 Maurice Blanchot, 'L'athéisme et l'écriture, L'humanisme et le cri', *L'Entretien infini*, pp. 367–93. Relevant reflection is also found in Richard Kearney, *Anatheism: Returning to God after God* (New York: Columbia University Press, 2009) and Jean-Luc Nancy, 'L'athéisme, essence des monothéismes', Entretien avec Jérôme-Alexandre Nielsberg, *Les Lettres françaises*, nouvelle série n° 15, 24 mai 2005.

Chapter 4

1 Maurice Blanchot, *Le pas au-delà* (Paris: Gallimard, 1973).
2 Augustine, *Confessions*, Book XI.vii and IV.x. For a critical treatment interpreting Augustine's thought on time and integrating it with the terms of French poststructuralist thought, see Karmen MacKendrick,

Fragmentation and Memory: Meditations on Christian Doctrine (New York: Fordham University Press, 2008), which is, on this topic, an extension of her reflections in *Immemorial Silence* (Albany: SUNY Press, 2001).

3 Rudolph Otto, *Das Heilige: Über das Irrationale in der Idee des Göttlichen und sein Verhältnis zum Rationalen* (Gotha: Leopold Klotz, 1926).

4 For contemporary philosophical reflections on the 'relocation of transcendence in immanence', one can consult John D. Caputo and Michael J. Scanlon, eds *Transcendence and Beyond* (Bloomington: Indiana University Press, 2007). Essays in Regina Schwartz, ed., *Transcendence: Philosophy, Literature, and Theology Approach the Beyond* (New York: Routledge, 2004) similarly stress the inherence of transcendence in immanence. James Faulconer, ed., *Transcendence in Philosophy and Religion* (Bloomington: Indiana University Press, 2003) explores the inscription of transcendence phenomenologically within the world and experience. The issue is acute already in medieval philosophy, as shown by Ruedi Imbach, *Deus est Intelligere: Das Verhältnis von Sein und Denken und seiner Bedeutung für das Gottesverständnis bei Thomas von Aquin und in den Pariser Quaestionen Meister Eckharts* (Freiburg Schweiz: Universitätsverlag, 1976), especially pp. 202–11, and is key to Imbach's situating of Dante in philosophical history in *Dante, la philosophie et les laics* (Fribourg: Éditions Universitaires Fribourg Suisse, 1996).

5 Cf. Dante, *De vulgari eloquentia* I.xvi.2: 'sicut in numero cuncta mensurantur ab uno'.

6 One line of such criticism runs from John Freccero to Marguerite Mills Chiarenza, 'The Imageless Vision and Dante's *Paradiso*', *Dante Studies* 90 (1972): 109–24.

7 James Miller, ed., *Dante and the Unorthodox: The Aesthetics of Transgression* (Canada: Wilfrid Laurier University Press, 2005), p. 2.

8 The rhetorical richness of the ineffability topos has been illuminated with mounting intensity by numerous critics including Giuseppe

Ledda, *Le guerra della lingua: Ineffabilità, retorica e narrativa nella Commedia di Dante* (Ravenna: Longo, 2002); Domenico Cofano, *La rettorica del silenzio nella Divina Comedia* (Bari: Palomar, 2003); A. Vallone, 'Il silenzio in Dante', in *La retorica del silenzio: Atti del Convegno Internazionale, Lecci, 24-27 Ottobre, 1991*, ed. C. A. Augieri (Lecce: Milella, 1994); R. D'Alfonso, *Il dialogo con Dio nella DC* (Bologna: Cleb, 1988).

9 One excellent introduction to the *Paradiso*'s poetics of ineffability is Anders Cullhed, 'Dicendo questo. A Note on Dante's Writing of Paradise', in *Dante: A Critical Reappraisal*, ed. Unn Falkeid (Oslo: Oslo Academic Press Unipub, 2008), pp. 35-45.

10 Among Dante's commentators, Giuseppe Mazzotta, in *Dante's Vision and the Circle of Knowledge* (Princeton: Princeton University Press, 1993), stresses his poetic epistemology and Baranski, *Dante e i segni: Saggi per una storia intellettuale di Dante Alighieri* (Naples: Liguori, 2000), particularly pp. 27-34 on 'Dante e le epistemologie medievali', calls this his preference for 'symbolic' over scientific discourse.

11 This range can be gauged by the distances between Jeremy Tambling, *Dante and Difference: Writing in the Commedia* (Cambridge: Cambridge University Press, 1988) or John Leavey, 'Derrida and Dante: Differance and the Eagle in the Sphere of Jupiter', *MLN* 91/1 (1976): 60-8 and Francis J. Ambrosio, *Dante and Derrida: Face to Face* (Albany: State University of New York Press, 2007).

12 I began to address this transition in 'Dante's Address to the Reader *en face* Derrida's Critique of Ontology', *Analecta Husserliana: The Yearbook of Phenomenological Research* LXIX (2000): 119-31.

13 For this conjunction, see especially Michael A. Sells, *Mystical Languages of Unsaying* (Chicago: University of Chicago Press, 1994).

14 A turn to the ineffable beyond language can be found already implicit in Aquinas himself, when read linguistically and poetically, as by Olivier-Thomas Venard, *Thomas d'Aquin poète-théologien* (Geneva: Ad Solem, 2002-09), 3 vols.

Chapter 5

1. Cf. Christophe Bident, 'The Movements of the Neuter', in *After Blanchot: Literature, Criticism, Philosophy*, eds Leslie Hill, Brian Nelson and Dimitris Vardoulakis (Newark: University of Delaware Press, 2004), pp. 13-34.
2. Blanchot, 'François Mauriac et ce qui était perdu', *La Revue française* 26 (1931).
3. Roland Barthes, *Le neutre: Cours au Collège de France (1977-78)* (Paris: Seuil, 2002), trans. Rosalind E. Krauss as *The Neutral: Lecture Course at the Collège de France (1977-1978)* (New York: Columbia University Press, 2007). An audio recording of the whole series of lectures is available online at http://www.ubu.com/sound/barthes.html.
4. See especially Milbank's *Being Reconciled: Ontology and Pardon* (London: Routledge, 2003).

Chapter 6

1. In his commentary on the *Paradiso*, Hollander points to, without presuming to resolve, the 'difficulty of understanding why Dante might have wanted to present himself as *forgetting* the greatest insight he (or practically anyone) has ever had ' (p. 837).
2. Georg Rabuse, 'Un punto solo m'è maggior letargo', *Deutsches Dante-Jahrbuch* 43 (1965): 138-52 develops this connection. Rabuse also produces abundant evidence from early commentators like Benvenuto that *letargo* in fact means 'infirmitas memoriae' or forgetting ('dimenticanza'), in a sense related to falling asleep ('assopimento'), and shows from evidence internal to the poem that the single 'point', which overwhelms Dante in his final vision is not just a moment or 'point' in time but God himself.
3. 'Oublieuse Mémoire', *L'entretien infini*, p. 459ff.

4 'L' oubli, la déraison', *L'entretien infini*, p. 289.
5 Nicholas Cusanus, *De visio Dei* in *Nicolai de Cusa Opera Omnia* (Leipzig: Meiner, 1932–2006). This is consistent with – and an extension of – Aquinas's and Augustine's view that theology is primarily God's own self-knowledge.
6 Frances A. Yates, *The Art of Memory* (Chicago: University of Chicago Press, 1966), p. 95.
7 Ernst Robert Curtius, *Europäische Literatur und Lateinsiches Mittelalter* (Bern: Francke, 1948), trans. Willard R. Trask as *European Literature and the Latin Middle Ages* (New York: Bollingen, 1952).
8 Weinrich mentions specifically Friedrich Ohly, *Bemerkungen eines Philologen zur Memoria* and Karl August Ott, 'Die Bedeutung der Mnemnotechnik für die Aufbau der *Divina Commedia*', *Deutches-Dante Jahrbuch* 62 (1987): 163–93. Subsequent refinement of this line of inquiry is proposed by Roberto Antonelli, '*Memoria rerum* et *memoria verborum*. La costruzione della *Divina Commedia*', *Criticón* 87-88-89 (2003): 35–45.
9 Weinrich, 'La mémoire linguistique de l'Europe', *Languages* 114 (1994): 13–24, citation, 16.
10 Harald Weinrich, *Lethe: Kunst und Kritik des Vergessens* (Munich: Beck, 1997), chapter 5, pp. 40–57; citation, p. 41.
11 Daniela Baroncini, 'Dante e la retorica dell'oblio', *Leitmotiv* 1 (2001): 9–19 (http://www.ledonline.it/leitmotiv/) traces the motif of forgetting all through Dante's *oeuvre* to its climax in the *Paradiso*. She points to the relevance of Blanchot in note 29. Also highlighting the *crisis* of memory in the mystical discourse of the *Paradiso* is Aldo Vallone, *Cultura e memoria in Dante* (Naples: Guida, 1988).
12 Umberto Eco, 'An Ars Oblivionalis? Forget It', trans. Marilyn Migiel, *PMLA* 103/3 (1988): 254–61.
13 Marc Augé, *Les formes de l'oubli* (Paris: Payot & Rivages, 1998), pp. 7 and 47.
14 Paul Ricoeur, *La mémoire, l'histoire, l'oubli* (Paris: Seuil, 2000), p. 536.
15 Jean-Louis Chrétien, *L'inoubliable et l'inespéré* (Paris: Desclée de Brouwer, 2000), p. 10.

Chapter 7

1. Jacques Derrida, 'Le supplément d' origine', *La voix et le phénomène* (Paris: P.U.F., 1967).
2. 'Parler, ce n' est pas voir', *L'entretien infini*, p. 40.
3. Augustine imagines senses that do not see or hear or taste or smell or touch corporeally also in *Confessions* X.vi.8.
4. Hans-Georg Gadamer, 'Wort und Bild – "so wahr, so seiend"' (1992), in *Gesammelte Werke*. vol. 8 (Tübingen: Mohr, 1981-).
5. Marlène Zarader, *L'être et le neuter: À partir de Maurice Blanchot* (Lagrasse: Verdier, 2001) traces Blanchot's rejection of Western ontology, especially as re-elaborated in the philosophies of Hegel, Husserl and Heidegger, in developing his counter theory of the 'night', especially 'the other night' (*l'autre nuit*) and the 'neuter'.
6. Dante criticism, too, has found this vision of no-thing at the heart of his vision of God. See especially Christian Moevs, *The Metaphysics of Dante's Comedy* (Oxford: Oxford University Press, 2005) and Rubina Giorgi, *Dante e Meister Eckhart per il tempo della fine* (Salerno: Ripostes, 1987).
7. Jean-Luc Marion's 'saturated phenomenon', in *De surcroît: Études sur les phénomènes saturés* (Paris: Presses Universitaires de France, 2001), similarly causes such a 'hyper-blindness' due to excess rather than defect in a seeing that exceeds its own limits.
8. Critique of idolatry is traced from ancient religions to modern philosophies by Moshe Halbertal and Avishai Margalit, *Idolatry*, trans. from Hebrew by Naomi Goldblum (Cambridge: Harvard University Press, 1992).
9. Cf. Marion's *L'idol et la distance: Cinque études* (Paris: Grasset, 1977), chapter 4 on Dionysius.
10. *L'espace littéraire* (Paris: Gallimard, 1955), pp. 370–1.
11. See, for example, Amador Vega, *Arte y santidad. Cuatro lecciones de estética apofática* (Pamplona: Universidad Pública de Navarra, 2005).

12 Jean Pfeiffer, 'L' expérience de Maurice Blanchot', *Empédocle* 11 (1950): 55–64, citation p. 56.
13 'De l'angoisse au langage' in *Faux pas* (Paris: Gallimard, 1943), p. 11.
14 See also reflections on the shattering epochal implications of Dante's title as a reversal of the ancient tragic worldview in Giorgio Agamben, 'Commedìa', in *Categorie italiane* (Venice: Marsilio, 1996), pp. 3–27.
15 'La question la plus profonde', *L'Entretien infini*, pp. 12–34.
16 See especially *L'écriture du désastre* (Paris: Gallimard, 1980), trans. Ann Smock as *The Writing of the Disaster* (Lincoln: University of Nebraska, 1995).
17 Bruno Forte, *La porta della bellezza. Per una estetica teologica* (Brescia: Morcelliana, 1999), p. 8. V. Melchiorre, 'L' analogia come chiave della creazione', *Rivista di filosofia neo-scolastica* 84 (1992): 563–88, similarly treats analogy in this tradition as a negative way safeguarding divine transcendence from every 'de-termination'.

Chapter 8

1 See especially Dionysius's *The Mystical Theology*, chapter 1 ('The Divine Darkness') and the anonymous, fourteenth-century *The Cloud of Unknowing*.

Chapter 9

1 Blanchot, 'René Char et la poésie du neutre', *L'entretien infini*, p. 442.
2 This paradoxical focus of negative theology on the flesh has been emphasized effectively by Emmanuel Falque, *Dieu, la chair et l'autre: d'Irénée à Duns Scot* (Paris: Presses Universitaires de France, 2008), as well as by *Apophatic Bodies: Negative Theology, Incarnation, and*

Relationality, eds Chris Boesel and Catherine Keller (New York: Fordham University Press, 2009) and by *Silence and the Word: Negative Theology and Incarnation*, eds Oliver Davies and Denys Turner (Cambridge: Cambridge University Press, 2002). Concerning specifically Dante, see Giuliana Carugati, *Il ragionare della carne: Dall'anima mundi a Beatrice* (Lecce: Manni, 2004).

Chapter 10

1 Hart, *The Dark Gaze*, p. 13, quoting Blanchot, *The Unavowable Community*, trans. Pierre Joris (Barrytown, N.Y.: Station Hill Press, 1988), p. 52; *La communauté inavouable* (Paris: Minuit, 1983), p. 87.

2 The negative theological function of Dante's Beatrice is signalled by Antonio Rossini, *Il Dante sappienziale: Dionigi e la bellezza di Beatrice* (Pisa: F. Serra, 2009), following the lead of the apophatic aesthetic theology of Hans Urs von Balthasar in *Herrlichkeit. Eine theologische Ästhetik* (Einsiedeln: Johannes Verlag, 1962), vol. II: Fächer der Stile, pt. 2. That Beatrice's beauty is a (negative) way to divine Truth is the theme also of Maurizio Malaguti, 'In trasparenza: La bellezza come via alla verità. Percorsi nel *Paradiso* di Dante', *Filosofi d'oggi per Dante* (Ravenna: Longo, 2005), ed. Nadia Ancarani, *Letture classensi* 32–4: 109–29.

3 In *Convivio* II.xiii.27, Dante observes that a point is indivisible and consequently cannot be measured. God is focused as 'point' in the *Paradiso* by Christian Moevs, '"Il punto che mi vinse": Incarnation, Revelation, and Self-Knowledge in Dante's *Commedia*', in *Dante's 'Commedia': Theology as Poetry*, eds Vittorio Montemaggi and Matthew Treherne (Notre Dame: University of Notre Dame Press, 2010), pp. 267–85.

4 Walter Rehm, *Orpheus: Der Dichter und die Toten* (Düsseldorf: Schwann, 1950).

5 Richard Kearney, *Strangers, Gods, Monsters: Interpreting Otherness* (New York: Routledge, 2003) makes this argument suggestively.

Chapter 11

1 Maurice Blanchot, *Thomas l'obscur* (Paris: Gallimard, 1941), p. 17.
2 Kevin Hart, *The Dark Gaze*, p. 12. The passage is first cited in full by Georges Bataille at the beginning of Part IV of *Inner Experience*, pp. 119–20.
3 Hart, p. 13, quoting Blanchot, 'The essential solitude', *L'espace littéraire*, p. 29. Jean-Luc Marion, *Etant donné: Essai d'une phénoménologie de la donation* (Paris: PUF, 1997), speaks in relation to the icon of a counter-gaze that inverts 'my' gaze.
4 Laurens ten Kate, 'Parole de contrainte, parole de contagion', in *Georges Bataille et la fiction*, ed. Jan Versteeg and Hank Hillenaar (Amsterdam: Rodopi, 1992), p. 19.
5 Blanchot works from this motif in *L'écriture du désastre*.

Chapter 12

1 However, in 'La révélation de Dante', *Chroniques Littéraires du Journal des Débats avril 1941–août 1944*, ed. Christophe Bident (Paris: Gallimard, 2007), pp. 159–64, Blanchot eulogistically remarks: 'But the *Divine Comedy* can sustain even excessive admiration.... One will never attribute to it as much as it gives' ('Mais la *Divine Comédie* supporte même l'excès dans l'admiration.... On ne lui prêtera jamais autant qu'elle donne', p. 160). Blanchot's critique of implacable reiteration of one's own dogmatic convictions is turned rather against Dmitri Merejkovsky, whose *Dante*, translated into French by Jean Chezeville (Albin Michel, 1940), presents Dante as Joachimite prophet and religious reformer seen in a perspective of Russian apocalypticism.
2 Erich Auerbach, *Dante als Dichter der irdischen Welt* (Berlin: Walter de Gruyter, 1929), trans. by Ralph Manheim as *Dante: Poet of the Secular World* (Chicago: University of Chicago Press, 1961). Ugo Dotti, *La Divina Commedia e la città dell'uomo: Introduzione alla lettura di Dante* (Rome: Donzelli, 1996) similarly defines the poem as 'an affirmation of the immanent in spite of its transcendent frame' (p. 8).

3   Blanchot on transgression is treated by some of his most noted interpreters, including Michael Holland, Jill Robbins, Vivian Liska, Gerald L. Bruns and Philippe Lacoue-Labarthe, in *The Power of Contestation: Perspectives on Maurice Blanchot*, eds Kevin Hart and Geoffrey H. Hartman (Baltimore: The Johns Hopkins University Press, 2004), as well as by John Gregg, *Maurice Blanchot and the Literature of Transgression* (Princeton: Princeton University Press, 1994).
4   Leslie Hill, introduction to *After Blanchot: Literature, Criticism, Philosophy*, eds Leslie Hill, Brian Nelson and Dimistris Vardoulakis (Newark: University of Delaware Press, 2004), pp. 1–2.
5   Giuseppe Mazzotta, 'Order and Transgression in the *Divine Comedy*', *Ideas of Order in the Middle Ages*, ed. W. Ginsberg (Binghamton: SUNY Binghamton Press, 1990): 1–21, citation, p. 19.

Chapter 13

1   Mazzotta, review of *Dante and the Unorthodox: The Aesthetics of Transgression* in *University of Toronto Quarterly* 76/1 (2007): 380.
2   *Dante's Vision and the Circle of Knowledge*, chapter 11: 'Theologia Ludens'.
3   Mazzotta, 'The Heaven of the Sun: Dante between Aquinas and Bonaventure', in *Dante for the New Millennium*, eds Teodolinda Barolini and H. Wayne Storey (New York: Fordham University Press, 2003), p. 166.
4   Mazzotta, 'Order and Transgression in the *Divine Comedy*'.

Chapter 14

1   Dante's anti-papal polemic has been key to the readings making him an anti-Catholic heretic, especially since Eugène Aroux, *Clef de la comédie anti-catholique de Dante Alighieri* (Carmagnola: Arktos, 1981

[1856]). Other parodic perspectives are suggested by Lino Pertile, *La puttana e il gigante: Dal Cantico dei cantici al Paradiso Terrestre di Dante* (Ravenna: Longo, 1998).

Chapter 15

1 Carlo Ruta, ed., *Poeti alla corte di Federico II. La scuola siciliana* (Rome: Di Renzo, 2003), reconstructs the historical milieu.

Chapter 17

1 Landmark works along this line of interpretation were cited in note 3 of Chapter 1. Distinguished among more recent contributions is Piero Vitellaro Zuccarello, et al., *Sotto il velame: Dante fra universalità esoterica e universalismo politico* (Milano: Mimesis, 2007).
2 A seminal impulse to the search for a 'sistema occulto' in the poem was given by Ugo Foscolo's *Discorso sul testo della Divina Commedia* (1825).
3 Robert Bonnell, *Dante le grand initié: Un message pour les temps futurs* (Paris: Dervy, 2002).
4 Adriano Lanza, *Dante eterodosso: Una diversa lettura della Commedia* (Bergamo: Moretti, 2004). See also Vincenzo Soro, 'Essenza gnostica del pensiero dantesco', chapter 5 in *La chiesa del Paracleto: Studi sullo Gnosticismo* (Todi: Atanòr, 1922).
5 Gregory B. Stone, *Dante's Pluralism and the Islamic Philosophy of Religion* (New York: Palgrave Macmillan, 2006).
6 For further explanation concerning theological revelation at the limits of human reason, see chapter I of *Poetry and Apocalypse: Theological Disclosures of Poetic Language* (Stanford: Stanford University Press, 2009). Dante's dynamic and philosophically enlightened conception of reason is placed in its medieval context by Didier Ottaviani, *La philosophie de la lumière chez Dante: Du Convivio à la Divine Comédie* (Paris: Campion, 2004).

Chapter 18

1. Slavoj Zizek's *The Puppet and the Dwarf: The Perverse Core of Christianity* (Cambridge: MIT Press, 2003) suggests in one way how this aspect of Christianity is resurfacing in our own time.
2. *Dante and the Church: Literary and Historical Essays*, eds Paolo Aquaviva and Jennifer Petrie (Dublin: Four Courts Press, 2007) documents historically the complexities and contradictions of Dante's relationship with the Church.
3. I develop this in 'The Rhetorical-Theological Presence of Romans in Dante: A Comparison of Methods in Philosophical Perspective', in *Medieval Readings of Romans*, eds William S. Campbell, Peter S. Hawkins and Brenda Dean Schildgen (New York: T&T Clark International, 2007), pp. 142–52.
4. I pursue this reflection further in 'The Coincidence of Reason and Revelation in Communicative Openness: A Critical Negative Theology of Dialogue', *Journal of Religion* 88/3 (2008): 365–92.
5. Gianni Vattimo, *Dopo la cristianità: Per un cristianesimo non religioso* (Milan: Garzanti, 2002), John D. Caputo, *The Weakness of God: A Theology of the Event* (Bloomington: Indiana University Press, 2006) and, above all, Jean-Luc Nancy, *L'Adoration* (Paris: Galilée, 2010), vol. 2 of *Déconstruction du christianisme*, effectively advocate a deconstructive Christianity or Christianity *as* deconstruction.
6. Illuminating in this regard is René Girard's reading of Job and Jesus in *La route antique des hommes pervers* (Paris: Bernard Grasset, 1985).
7. Maurizio Palma di Cesnola, *Semiotica Dantesca: Profetismo e diacronia* (Ravenna: Longo, 1995), p. 187. See also Andrea Cuccia, *Il pensiero esoterico nella* Commedia *di Dante* (Soveria: Rubettino, 2009): 'Il linguaggio segreto dei settari', pp. 75–92.

Part Three

1. George Steiner, *After Babel* (Oxford: Oxford University Press, 1975), a recurrent thesis.

Notes 193

Chapter 19

1 Michel Foucault, 'Préface à la transgression', *Critique* 195-6 (1963): 752.
2 See Zygmunt G. Baranski, 'Obscenity and Scatology in Dante', in *Dante for the New Millenium*, eds Teodolinda Barolini and Wayne Storey (New York: Fordham University Press, 2003), pp. 259-73.

Chapter 20

1 I have dealt with the privileging of experience as 'sole authority and sole value', from which Bataille's meditation begins, in Chapter III of *Poetry and Apocalypse*. There I follow the trajectory of this phenomenological revolution from Dante to James Joyce.
2 Peter Hawkins develops this reading in 'John Is with Me', in *Dante's Testaments*, pp. 54-71.
3 Georges Bataille, *L'expérience intérieure* (Paris: Gallimard, 1954 [1943]), p. 120.
4 Blanchot, 'Maître Eckhart' and 'Expérience Intérieure' in *Faux Pas* (Paris: Gallimard, 1943).
5 See, especially Alois M. Haas, 'Mystische Erfahrung und Sprache', in *Sermo mysticus: Studien zu Theologie und Sprache der deutschen Mystik* (Freiburg, Switzerland: Paulusdruckerei, 1979) and '*Mors mystica*: Thanatologie mer Mystik, inbesondere der deutschen Mystik', *Freiburger Zeitschrift für Philosphie und Theologie* 23/3 (1976): 304-92.
6 Achim Wurm, 'Mystisches Sprechen', in *Philosophie der UnVerbindlichkeit: Einführungen in ein austehendes Denken* (Würzburg: Königshausen und Neumann, 1995), p. 236.

Chapter 21

1 Cf. the 'liberi soggiacete' ('freely subjugated') of *Purg.* XVI.73.
2 For postmodern reinvestments of the sublime, see Jean-François Lyotard, *Leçons sur l'analytique du sublime* (Paris: Galilée, 1991).

3 Some good examples are considered by Marie-Chantal Killeen, *Essai sur l'indicible: Jabès, Blanchot, Duras* (Saint-Denis: Presses Universitaires de Vincennes, 2004).

Appendix

* This essay was published in preliminary form as 'The Ethical Vision of Dante's *Paradiso* in Light of Levinas', *Comparative Literature* 59/3 (2007): 209–27.

1 'La négativité de l'*In* de l'Infini – autrement qu' être, divine comédie – creuse un désir qui ne saurait se combler, qui se nourrit de son accroisssement même et qui s'exalte comme Désir – qui s' éloigne de sa satisfaction – dans la mesure où il s'approche du Désirable'. *De Dieu qui vient à l'idée* (Paris, Vrin, 1982), p. 111.

2 Ethics is so conceived in the Romantic philosophy of the youthful Hegel, Schelling and Hölderlin, according to whose 'Oldest System Program of German Idealism' (1796) all future metaphysics was to fall under ethics (' – *eine Ethik. Da die ganze Metaphysik künftig in die Moral fällt*'). G.W.F Hegel, 'Das älteste Systemprogramm des deutschen Idealismus'. *Werke*. Frankfurt a.M: Suhrkamp, 1971. Vol 1: *Frühe Schriften*, p. 234.

3 I refer particularly to Thomas Wiemar, *Die Passion des Sagens. Zur Deutung der Sprache bei E. Levinas und ihrer Realisierung im philosophischen Diskurs* (Freiburg/München: K. Alber, 1988) and Antje Kapust, *Berührung ohne Berührung: Ethik und Ontologie bei Merleau-Ponty und Levinas* (München: Wilhelm Fink, 1999). Somewhat comparable concerns and critique of Levinas may be found in Fabio Ciaramelli, 'Levinas's Ethical Discourse between Individuation and Universality', and in other essays in *Re-Reading Levinas*, eds Robert Bernasconi and Simon Critchley (Bloomington: Indiana University Press, 1991).

4 I am playing off the term 'objective correlative' coined by T. S. Eliot in his essay on *Hamlet*, in *Selected Essays* (London: Faber, 1951).

5 Emmanuel Levinas, 'La Trace de l'Autre', *Tijdschrift voor Philosophie* (September 1963), pp. 605-23, translated as 'The Trace of the Other', in *Deconstruction in Context: Literature and Philosophy*, pp. 345-59, ed. Mark C. Taylor (Chicago: University of Chicago Press, 1986).

6 That Dante's vision in paradise, in accordance with the premises of apophatic theology, must be essentially objectless has long been recognized by Dante scholarship, for example, Marguerite Mills Chiarenza, 'The Imageless Vision and Dante's *Paradiso*', *Dante Studies* 90 (1972): 109-24. Still, it is hard to keep this in mind in interpreting the poem, given the wealth of objective forms that it produces and displays; hence, the importance of the attempt to understand why and how Dante's vision is necessarily objectless. We require a strong interpretation of what this vision is, after all, if it is not vision of any object. Useful treatments of the subject include Peter S. Hawkins, 'Augustine, Dante, and the Dialectic of Ineffability' in *Dante's Testaments: Essays in Scriptural Imagination* (Stanford: Stanford University Press, 1999) and Steven Botterill, 'Mysticism and Meaning in Dante's *Paradiso*', in *Dante for the New Millenium*, eds Teodolinda Barolini and H. Wayne Storey (New York: Fordham University Press, 2003).

7 The third canticle – *Paradiso* – has been considered to be distinguished precisely by this 'objectivity', for example, by R. Montano, *Suggerimenti per una lettura di Dante* (Napoli: Quaderni di 'Delta', 1956): 'the Poet portrays scenes in their objective reality ... the attention of the one who writes is concentrated entirely on rendering something objective, real ... .' ('il Poeta ritrae le scene nella loro obiettiva realtà ... l'attenzione di chi scrive è interamente concentrata nella considerazione e nella resa di qualcosa di obiettivo, reale ... .').

8 In what follows, I quote and translate from Levinas's mature and radical formulation of his ideas in *Autrement qu'être et au-delà de l'essence* (Dordrecht: Kluwer, 1990 [1974]). Also constantly impinging on my representations of Levinas's thought is his *Totalité et infini: Essai sur l'extériorité* (Dordrecht: Kluwer, 1992 [1961]).

9 There is thus some basis (though not necessarily the one he suggests) for Jorge Luis Borges's observation that, 'There is a person who is missing in the *Comedia*, who could not be there because it would have been excessively human. This person is Jesus' ('Hay un personaje que falta en la *Comedia* y que no podía estar porque hubiera sido demasiado humano. Ese personaje es Jesús'). 'Siete noches' (1980), in *Obras completas* 1975–85 (Barcelona: Emecé, 1989), p. 211.
10 That Levinas is a proponent of neither Christianity nor mysticism makes this convergence all the more surprising and significant.
11 Especially revealing of this biblical grounding of Levinas's thought is his *L'au-delà du verset: Lectures et discours talmudiques* (Paris: Minuit, 1982).

Index

Abraham 125
absence, of work 85-7, 147-8
Adam 10-12, 21
Al-Farabi 120
Alain de Lille 108
analogy, as disanalogy 74-5
Anselm 108
apophatics 40, 45, 61
 and metaphysics 175
 and mysticism 136
Aquinas, Thomas 40, 46, 81, 174
Arachne 6
archetype 8, 10
Argo 47, 52, 95
Argonauts 12, 47-9
Aristotle 116, 143
Aroux, Eugène 5
ars memoria 54-6
Auerbach, Erich 100, 126
Augé, Marc 57
Augustine 19-20, 36, 55-6, 58, 74, 92, 107, 164, 167
Averroes 120

Balthasar, Hans Urs von 74
Barthes, Roland 6, 15
 and neuter 43-4
Bataille, Georges 6, 15, 34, 42, 96, 136-7
 and inner experience 139-42
 oeil révulsé 137
 restricted economy 108, 133
 sovereignty 147
Beatrice, reflection of divinity 88-91, 156
Bident, Christophe 42
Blanchot, Maurice 6, 15, 32-3, 42, 98-104, 134-6, 149
 and ancient fear 55-7
 and forgetting 49-52, 58
 and inner experience 140-1
 and literature 40
 as novelist 71, 95
 on seeing and saying 60-2
 and theology 38
Boethius 91, 108
Bonaventure 27, 48
Bonnefoy, Ives, the improbable 77-8
Bonnel, Robert 120
Bruno, Giordano 127
Brutus and Cassius 4

Cato 5
Ceasar 4
Char, René 78, 98-9
Chrétien, Jean-Louis 58-9
Christ, event 15, 124
 as Orpheus 91
Christianity 15, 74, 109, 120-1, 124-8, 140, 150
Clement of Alexandria 91, 149
comedy 71-2
Constantine, Donation of 111
contestation 136, 143, 150
Curtius, Ernst Robert 54
Cusa, Nicholas of 53, 96, 99, 127, 141, 143

deconstruction, of self- 20
 of Christianity and of signs 128, 149
Derrida 16, 34, 39, 43, 108-9
Dionysius the Areopagite 15, 20, 27, 44, 46, 51, 74
Divine Names 23
Dominic, Saint 4, 118

Eckhart, Meister 20, 40, 45-6, 81, 86, 99, 127, 141, 143
Eco, Umbeto 56

Elijah and Elisha 117
empire, Holy Roman 3, 114
Empyrean 22, 60, 138
Eriugena, John Scott 81
esoteric interpretation 5, 119–20, 127, 129–30, 146
eternity 36, 54, 102
  as temptation 100
ethics 151
  as first philosophy 152
Eurydice 89–91

failure, poetics of 29, 36, 38–9, 62, 69, 84–5, 87, 92, 136, 153, 167, 176
Folquet of Marseille 3
forgetting 22, 46–62, 68, 73, 78, 85, 98, 149
  lethe 51, 56
Forte, Bruno 74
Foucault, Michel 6, 134–7
Fra Dolcino 4
Francis, Saint 124
  Franciscans 4, 119
Frederick II 114–15

Gadamer x, 65
Geryon 7
Glaucus 8
Guénon, René 5

Hart, Kevin 16, 21, 89, 95, 141–2
Hegel 32, 69, 109
Heidegger x, 80, 98
heresy 3
  heterodoxy 6, 118–19, 128, 150
hermeneutics x, 40
  existential xi
  German xi
hierarchy 138
Hölderlin 69, 78, 98–9, 104
Hollander, Robert 33, 48

Ibn Arabi 120
Icarus 7, 148

idolatry 68
im-mediacy 66, 69
images, as veils 61
impossible 71, 96, 142, 145
incarnation 125, 170
ineffability 153–61
  as divinity 153
  Letter to Can Grande 158
  pen jumps 32, 36, 169
  topos xi–xii, 32, 38, 102
inner experience 76, 139–42
interdisciplinarity xiv

John of the Cross 141
  noche oscura 81
Jove, Heaven of 23–4, 103

Keats, John, negative capability 102–3
kenosis 102, 125, 144

language, as absolute 30
  experience of 36
  in its infinity 68
  linguistic turn 19–26
  metaphor of immediacy 27
  poetic 22
  vernacular 22
Lanza, Adriano 120
Levinas, Emmanuel 6, 151–4, 161–76
  illéité 174
  proximity 168
  'Saying' 154
  'signification' 165

Mallarmé, Stéphane 78, 99
  Igitur 80
Marsyas 7, 93
Mazzotta 101, 107–8
metaphor 38, 159
  for the Transcendent 167
Milbank 45
Miller, James 37
modernity 22
Moevs, Christian 96, 142

Index

Monarchy 45, 126
mysticism, apophatic 20, 40

Narcissus, redeemed 27
negative theology 15, 20, 31, 42, 76–81, 86, 96, 98, 102–4, 128, 135
  as affirmative 136
  via negativa 143
Neoplatonism 139
  and the One 37
Neptune 53–4
neuter 42–6, 62, 99
  definition 35, 42
  etymology 42
  of language 37, 41
  and negation 35
  as nuance 32
  non-oppositional 15
Nietzsche, madman 80–1, 149
night 51
  other night 90
  of unknowing 79
Nimrod 12
non-knowing 42, 104, 127
  non-experience 96, 142
  non-vision 96
Nyssa, Gregory of 44, 46

oltraggio 56, 135
Orpheus 83–8
  as Christ 92
  Renaissance and Romantic versions 92
other 131
  first 171
  for Levinas 161, 173
  as origin 164, 172
  as passion 163
outside (*Dehors*) 30, 35, 38, 61, 97, 146–7
Ovid 6, 92

Parmenides 162
Pascoli, Giovanni 5

Paul, antinomianism 125
  political authority 123
  raptus 13, 88, 171
  vas electionis 9
Phaethon 7, 148
Plato 69
  divided line 67
Plotinus 36, 58–9
poetry, as world-transforming 13–14
pope, as vicar 3, 111–12
  Hadrian V 138

reason, human 127, 131–2
  limits of 121
revelation, Christian 32, 47, 149
  as disclosedness 47
  divine 62, 112, 124, 126
  ethical 176
  as experience 142, 161, 168
  of limits 135
  metaphysical 167, 175
  negative 135
  re-veiling 61
  and representation xii, 167–8
  theological xiii, 15
  total 135
Ricoeur, Paul 57
Rilke, Rainer Maria 78, 92, 99
Rimbaud 131
Riphaeus 5
Rossetti, Dante Gabriel 5

sacred 69, 134–5, 144
sacrifice 81, 87, 148
  self- 141
self-referentiality 26–7
Semelè 170
shadowy prefaces 54, 61
Sibyl 22, 36, 47, 52, 61, 73, 93, 172
signs 19, 21
  transcendental signified 19–20
space of literature 71, 76, 97, 100
Steiner, George 131
step/not beyond 30, 35–41, 148

Stone, Gregory 120-1, 124, 126-7
subjective correlative 155

trace 57, 154-5
Trajan 5
transcendence 52, 176
   ethical relation to 173
   in immanence 36-7, 40,
      126-8, 145
   of language 36, 40, 63-5
   and law 145
   of representation 163
   of self 153
   of sense 25
   as signification 165
   of Trinity 27
   of vision 63-4
   witness to 161-71
transgression 139
   against self 146-7
   of Being 171
   etymology 29, 139
   non-oppositional 14, 100
   non-transgression 150
   and order 101, 145, 147
   of signs 149
   social and political 107-9
trasumanar 98, 127, 131, 149, 169
trauma 168-70
truth x, xiv
   absolute 126
   aletheia 51
   of being 171
   beyond presence 88
   deconstructive 128
   incommensurable 58
   interior 140
   literal 145
   rational 122, 131
   revealed 80, 116, 126
   total 53
   transcendent 127

Ulysses 8, 88, 117, 146-8
unworking (*désoeuvrement*) 61, 73,
   79-80, 148
Uzzah 112

Valli, Luigi 5
Verlaine, Paul 44
Virgil 7, 92
visibile parlare 23, 66
visio Dei 23, 53, 73, 93
Vita nuova 55

Weinrich, Harald 55-7
writing, experience of 76-82
   as disaster 97
   and exile 103
   and negative theology 86
Wurm, Achim 143

Yates, Frances 54

www.ingramcontent.com/pod-product-compliance
Lightning Source LLC
Chambersburg PA
CBHW072235290426
44111CB00012B/2107